Goebbels
and *Der Angriff*

Goebbels

and *Der Angriff*

RUSSEL LEMMONS

THE UNIVERSITY PRESS OF KENTUCKY

Scholarly publisher for the Commonwealth,
serving Bellarmine College, Berea College, Centre
College of Kentucky, Eastern Kentucky University,
The Filson Club, Georgetown College, Kentucky
Historical Society, Kentucky State University,
Morehead State University, Murray State University,
Northern Kentucky University, Transylvania University,
University of Kentucky, University of Louisville,
and Western Kentucky University.

Editorial and Sales Offices: Lexington, Kentucky 40508-4008

Library of Congress Cataloging-in-Publication Data

Lemmons, Russel
    Goebbels and Der Angriff / Russel Lemmons.
        p.   cm.
    Includes bibliographical references and index.
    ISBN 0-8131-1848-4 (acid-free paper)
    1. Goebbels, Joseph, 1897-1945. 2. Angriff. 3. National
socialists—Biography. 4. Propaganda, German—History—20th
century. 5. Germany—Politics and government—1933-1945. 6. Public
opinion—Germany. I. Title.
DD247.G6L46 1994
943.085—dc20   93-33405

This book is dedicated to my wife,
Diana,
with all my love.

Contents

Acknowledgments   ix

Introduction   1

1. The Berlin NSDAP before *Der Angriff*, 1920-1927   6

2. An Institutional History of *Der Angriff*, 1927-1933   21

3. The Party, the Fuehrer Myth, and the
        Presidential Election   43

4. The SA and Political Violence   65

5. Appeals to the Proletariat   89

6. The "System"   111

Conclusion   128

Notes   132

Bibliography   160

Index   168

Acknowledgments

Since this book began as a doctoral dissertation at Miami University, I must begin by thanking my *Doktorvater*, Professor Jay W. Baird, who introduced me to Goebbels's newspaper. He has served as a model not only of an excellent scholar but also, more important, of a fine human being. I would be remiss if I did not also thank Professor Wolfgang Wippermann, who served as my ersatz *Doktorvater* during my stay in Berlin. The assiduous work of my dissertation readers, Professors Robert Thurston, Allan Winkler, and Ruth Sanders is also appreciated. This book would have been impossible to complete without the generous support of the Fulbright Commission, which enabled me to do research in Germany. During my stay in the Federal Republic, I benefited from the help of the staffs of numerous libraries and archives: the Staatsbibliothek Berlin, the Berlin Document Center, the Landesarchiv Berlin, the Geheimes Staatsarchiv preussischer Kulturbesitz, the Bundesarchiv, and the Instutut fuer Zietgeschichte. New Mexico Highlands University provided the funds for a research trip to California, and I must also express my appreciation to the staff of the Hoover Institution on War, Revolution and Peace. The staff of the Miami University inter-library loan office was always courteous and helpful. The moral support of my colleagues at NMHU is also appreciated, as are the diligent efforts of my graduate assistant, Louis Gonzales, whose hard work provided me with the time needed to complete revisions. I must also express my gratitude to the Rodens, Davidsons, and Tim Anderson, who saw me through some difficult times in Germany, and my parents, who were always supportive of my work. Most important, I thank my wife, Diana, who tolerated a ten-month separation while I was doing the research for this project. Her love has been an important foundation of my life.

Introduction

Scholars remain intrigued by the "totalitarian" regimes of the twentieth century, especially those of Germany and the Soviet Union. They have, for the past forty years, repeatedly tried to explain how the governments of Hitler and Stalin functioned and why they maintained so much public support in the face of the atrocities they committed. What is even more inexplicable is the fact that both the Nazis and the Bolsheviks seized power from governments that promised their citizens a great deal of personal freedom. Why did the German and Russian people willingly surrender the rights guaranteed by these governments and entrust their fortunes to regimes that tried completely to control their lives?

In pursuing answers to this question, historians have naturally turned to the study of Nazi and Leninist propaganda techniques. Works by Ernest K. Bramsted, Jay W. Baird, Robert Herzstein, Ian Kershaw, David Welsh, and W.A. Boelcke have dealt with this subject from the German perspective.[1]

These books share two important characteristics. First, all of them are concerned primarily with the period after the Nazis came to power and say little regarding Nazi propaganda during the *Kampfzeit* (time of struggle). Secondly, the National Socialist Press, aside from Oron Hale's *The Captive Press in the Third Reich*, has been, until quite recently, largely ignored. The publication of books by Dennis Showalter, William Combs, and Norbert Frei and Johannes Schmitz, as well as Peter

Stein's important bibliography, *Die NS Gaupresse 1925-1933*, are a beginning in the filling of this historiographical gap. Once again, however, with the exception of Stein's and Showalter's books, these works are concerned primarily with the period after 1933. Much work remains to be done.[2]

This study is not only concerned with pre-1933 Nazi propaganda but also, more specifically, with the impact of a newspaper in spreading Nazi ideas. It deals with the role of Goebbels's Berlin organ, *Der Angriff*, in his battles with the Weimar "system" as well as German Communism. The period under consideration—often called the "Blood Years" by the Nazis—encompasses events from the establishment of the newspaper in July 1927 until the Nazi "seizure of power" in January 1933.

The primary function of *Der Angriff* was to attack National Socialism's political enemies. For Goebbels and the editors of the newspaper, the Jews, the creators of both Bolshevism and democracy, were the primary enemy. A violent anti-Semitism permeated the pages of *Der Angrif*, and the Jews became the scapegoat for all of Germany's, indeed the world's, problems.

According to *Der Angriff*, the main force confronting the "world Jewish conspiracy" was the National Socialist German Workers' Party (NSDAP) and its front-line troops, the Sturmabteilung (SA). The SA, composed of at first hundreds and later thousands of unemployed working-class youths, became a crusader against Jewry and its revolutionary force, Marxism. A section of *Der Angriff*, "Kampf um Berlin," was dedicated to reporting the violent street clashes between the SA and the Rotfrontkaempferbund or RFB (the paramilitary organization of the German Communist Party or KPD). SA men injured or killed in the struggle for the control of Berlin's streets became heroes on the pages of the Berlin newspaper. Horst Wessel, murdered by the KPD in 1930, became the archetypical Nazi hero. Much of the legend concerning his personality and exploits—a major chapter in Nazi mythology—began on the pages of *Der Angriff*. It was the system, created by the "November Criminals," which the Berlin paper held responsible for the deaths of Wessel and other Germans in the struggle against the Jews. *Der Angriff* played a vital role in this battle with the system. Oron Hale, in his *The Captive Press in the Third Reich*, dismisses Goebbels's foray into newspaper publishing as totally ineffective. He claims that "as an afternoon journal it never achieved a large circulation" and that "Goebbels' reputation as a militant Gauleiter and master propagandist should not be extended to newspaper editing and publishing." My research, however, indicates that, in reality, *Der Angriff* played a much more important role in the rise of National Socialism in Berlin than Hale allows.[3]

In order to establish the importance of *Der Angriff*, I will have to address various issues and answer a number of questions. How did the newspaper serve as a forum for Nazi ideas? What were these ideas? What was its role in internal party struggles? How did it depict the battle in the streets between the SA and the RFB? How effective was the Nazi press as a campaign tool? At whom was *Der Angriff's* propaganda aimed? Who read the newspaper? How did the Weimar government respond to its attacks? My work deals with all of these questions in trying to determine the role of the newspaper in the emergence of National Socialism in Berlin.

In addition, my research makes a contribution to two other major historiographical debates. The first of these has to do with the nature of Nazi ideology. Was it the product of a basically antimodernist world view, or was it simply a new way of embracing modernity? Though the fact that the Nazis were willing to make use of a newspaper in their propaganda may seem to suggest that the Nazis accepted the world of the twentieth century, a careful examination of the copy contained in *Der Angriff* forces one to come to a different conclusion. National Socialism contained a vibrant antimodernist component.

Traditionally, historians have argued that, following a poor showing in the May 1928 elections, there was a dramatic shift in the focus of the NSDAP's propaganda. Before this date, the Nazis aimed their propaganda primarily at Germany's working classes, hoping to compete with the Communists and Socialists. Supposedly realizing that the majority of their meager support came from the countryside, the Nazi leadership decided to shift its propaganda focus to appeals to the peasantry. A careful examination of *Der Angriff's* copy both before and after May 1928 indicates that the situation was, in fact, much more complicated than this, with local leaders having extensive control over the propaganda lines they pursued. The Nazis did not give up on the proletariat after the spring of 1928.

Further, *Der Angriff* is of interest because it provided Goebbels with his first opportunity to develop many of the propaganda techniques he would use during the Third Reich. Such themes as the "Unknown SA Man" and the "myth of resurrection and return" made their first appearance on the pages of this newspaper. A study of *Der Angriff* is vital to understanding subsequent developments in Nazi mythology.

Finally, this study will attempt a partial explanation regarding why many Germans were willing to place their nation in the hands of anti-Semitic thugs totally without experience in government. By 1930, the economic collapse of Europe had placed Germany in such a dire situation that many people were willing to turn to anyone who promised to relieve their distress. Part of the appeal of the Nazis (as well as the German Communist Party) was that they openly professed that they would do whatever was necessary to end the economic depression. *Der Angriff* played a vital role not only in placing the Nazis in a positive light but also in attacking the Weimar Republic, convincing millions of Germans that democratic government (controlled by the Jews) was at the root of Germany's problems.

A Fulbright-Hays Grant aided in the completion of the research for this project. A ten-month stay in West Berlin provided opportunities to visit all of the major archives with holdings concerning *Der Angriff*. This is particularly important when one considers the scarcity of secondary evidence on this subject. Aside from Hans-Georg Raehm's pro-Nazi and largely propagandistic *"Der Angriff," 1927-1930: Der nationalsozialistische Typ der Kampfzeit*, there is no major secondary work dealing with *Der Angriff*. Bramsted's book on National Socialist propaganda and Helmut Heiber's biography of Goebbels touch upon the subject only in passing. Therefore, the bulk of this project is based upon archival sources.[4] A note on organization is also appropriate. The first two chapters deal with the period before the creation of *Der Angriff* and the institutional history of the paper respectively. They are organized, for the most part, chronologically. The next four chapters are concerned with the major propaganda themes pursued in the paper. Because of the subject matter, they are organized thematically. The final chapter deals with *Der Angriff* and the law. Noticeably absent from this work is a chapter dealing specifically with anti-Semitism. This is a function of the contention made here that anti-Semitism was at the root of *all Der Angriff's* propaganda. To single out anti-Semitism as a separate phenomenon would therefore be artificial and make it appear that it was only one aspect of Goebbels's propaganda.

Because of the issues raised, this study should contribute to the literature on the rise of National Socialism. No major secondary work has been published on the history of Gau Berlin before 1933. These frenetic years saw numerous political parades, speakers haranguing people in the streets, and battles—often ending in death—between political factions. Joseph Goebbels also began his foray into political propaganda. All these incidents can be seen on the pages of *Der Angriff*.

1

The Berlin NSDAP before *Der Angriff,* 1920-1927

Chaos characterized the early history of National Socialism in Berlin. Promoted by the atmosphere of the capital after the revolution of November 1918, the party emerged as one of numerous *voelkisch* (far right) groups determined to destroy the fledgling republic. Because of the fragmented nature of right-wing politics during this period, the origins of National Socialism in Berlin are extremely difficult to trace, but 1920 appears to be an appropriate point of departure. In that year, a chapter of the repugnant Jew-baiter Julius Streicher's German Socialist Party or DSP (Deutschsozialistischen Partei) was founded in the capital city. The following year this group renamed itself National Socialists (Streicher Group).[1]

November 1922 saw the establishment of the first Ortsgruppe Berlin der NSDAP (Local Branch of the Berlin NSDAP) at the Restaurant Reichskanzler in Kreuzberg. This group, however, was short-lived. The murder of Foreign Minister Walther Rathenau by right-wing extremists had led to passage of the Republikschutzgesetz (Law for the Defense of the Republic) under which Prussian Interior Minister Carl Severing had outlawed numerous political parties aimed at the violent overthrow of German democracy. Among those receiving a *Verbot* (prohibition) in Prussia was the NSDAP. Therefore, the newly formed Nazi organization called itself the Grossdeutschen Arbeiterpartei (Greater-German Workers' Party) or GDAP. The title of the new group did not mask its political goals, and Severing banned the party on 10 January 1923. The National Socialist movement in Berlin would not reemerge until after the ill-fated Beer Hall Putsch and Adolf Hitler's release from prison.[2]

Although a party organization was not permitted during the years 1923-1925, the evolution of the groups that would become the paramilitary wing of the NSDAP, the Sturmabteilungen (Storm Sections), or SA, continued. The period 1921-1923 witnessed the genesis of the so-called Voelkische Turnerschaften (People's Gymnastic Groups). Mere fronts for rightwing hooliganism, these clubs were important forerunners of the SA and engaged in the burgeoning civil war in the streets of Berlin. For example, in April 1924, members of the Turnerschaft Hutten, on their way to a political rally in the Bluethnersaele on Luetzowplatz, brawled with members of the German Communist Party (KPD), both sides suffering numerous injuries. Even before the April clash with the KPD, the Turnerschaften were being absorbed by the newly founded Frontbann. This group, led in the north by the former SA chief, Ernst Roehm, would play an important role in the development of the Berlin SA. By March 1925, the Frontbann Berlin-Brandenburg had two thousand members.[3]

About this time, the Frontbann formed an alliance with the newly reestablished Ortsgruppe Berlin of the NSDAP. On 17 February 1925, ten days before Hitler officially reestablished the Nazi Party, Erich Thimm founded the new National Socialist group. The following month, Hitler upgraded the organization to the Gau Gross-Berlin der NSDAP (Greater-Berlin Region of the NSDAP), which included the entire province of Brandenburg. The Fuehrer also named Dr. Ernst Schlange the first Gauleiter (regional leader) of Berlin's 350 Nazis.[4]

For the first month of the party's existence, it maintained close ties with the Frontbann, portions of which served as the paramilitary arm of the NSDAP. Since most of the Frontbann insisted upon maintaining its independence from the Nazis, pressure grew within the party to sever ties with the organization. The split between the Nazi movement and the Frontbann as well as the founding of the Berlin SA occurred on 22 March 1926. On this date, the leadership of the Berlin Frontbann met in the Wernicke bar on Potsdamerstrasse. Kurt Daluege led the faction, which included about one-fifth (450 men) of the Frontbann, that seceded and offered its allegiance to the Nazis, forming the core of the new SA. The remaining 80 percent gave its support to Erich Ludendorff's Tannenbergbund, one of numerous other extreme nationalist groups in Weimar Germany. In June, the NSDAP announced that membership in the Frontbann was not a substitute for belonging to the SA.[5]

In spite of the creation of the SA and the upgrading of the local organization to Gau status, the movement did not prosper. Intra-party strife and political impotence infested the party organization. The bone of contention in these disagreements was one not of party program but of power. The Nazis divided into two factions, one supporting Gauleiter Schlange, the other behind SA leader Daluege. In August 1926, Berlin's 120 district leaders met in the Haberlandt Hall to discuss the Gau leadership post. The Daluege faction had shrewdly waited until Schlange was on vacation to make its move. The opening of the meeting foreshadowed subsequent events. The introductory remarks made by the temporary Gauleiter, Erich Schmiedecke, were, as the official Situation Report recorded, "interrupted by noise and interruptions coming from the majority of those present." Daluege then took action. Claiming that both Schlange and Schmiedecke were corrupt, he insisted that they be called before the party's Court of Honor. The leader of the Berlin Court of Honor, a man identified only as Hageinan, argued that Schmiedecke should resign in light of the charges brought against him and that a committee should be established to run the Gau. The Berlin SS chief, Wolter, claiming authority from Hitler, removed Schmiedecke and made Knodn acting Gau Leader. In addition, the regional leaders voted to establish a committee to oversee the Gau. This is the first example of the rift between the SA and the party leadership that would come to characterize Gau Berlin in the 1930s. Given the anarchy within the party, it is small wonder that much of the Berlin party leadership enthusiastically greeted the appointment of Joseph Goebbels as Gauleiter in October 1926.[6]

Goebbels earned his reputation as an effective organizer in the Ruhr Valley. An excellent speaker, his "leftist" views enabled him to appeal to the working class of the heavily industrialized region. He worked his way up the party hierarchy as a protégé of Gregor Strasser, who, along with his brother Otto, ran a *voelkisch* publishing house, Kampfverlag, in Berlin. The Strassers were notorious within the movement for their somewhat unorthodox views—they took the word "socialism" in the party's title seriously—and quarreled often with Hitler. Goebbels's connection with the Strassers both helped and hindered his appointment as leader of the Berlin Nazis. Though it was clear that his anticapitalist views would aid in his mission to the largely working-class Berlin populace, Hitler was hesitant to appoint a potential dissident to such an important post.[7]

During the course of 1926, this impediment was removed. Goebbels's conversion to blind support of Hitler, which would take years, began at this time. Even after breaking with the Strassers, he was often critical of his Fuehrer. Political enemies, hoping to discredit Goebbels as an opportunist, probably misrepresented his actions at the Bamberg leadership conference of February 1926. In Bamberg, he allegedly broke completely with the Strassers and became an unquestioning supporter of Hitler. Goebbels's diaries paint a somewhat different picture. Here one sees hesitancy on his part. Although he clearly found Hitler's personality compelling, Goebbels frequently disagreed with the Fuehrer's program and was less willing to surrender his principles than his opponents claimed. Hence, it took several months for him to come around to support of Hitler.[8]

Goebbels's visit to Munich in April 1926 was probably when Hitler finally won him over. The Fuehrer treated him well, going out of his way to impress his visitor. Hitler extended Goebbels every courtesy, dining with him on a number of occasions and loaning him his car. On 13 April, Goebbels recorded his impressions of a meeting with Hitler: "We are moving much closer." He realized that his ideas and the Fuehrer's were not very different. Hitler also wanted to socialize "combines, trusts, production of finished articles, transport, etc." The ideological rift between them was becoming narrower. "I am reassured all around," he continued. "Taken all round he is a man. With his sparkling mind he can become my leader. I bow to his greatness, his political genius!" They parted friends, Goebbels now Hitler's consistent but by no means unquestioning ally.[9]

With the eruption of controversy in Berlin in the summer of 1926, a search for a new Gauleiter for the capital began. The party leadership considered Goebbels for the post. Probably because he recognized the inherent difficulties of going to Berlin, Goebbels was much more interested in a position in Munich as the party's general secretary, but he received neither position at this time.[10]

At the 1926 party congress in Weimar, the first at which the Berlin NSDAP was represented, the Berlin leadership began to court Goebbels for the Gauleiter post. Hitler offered him the job in August; in response, Goebbels "sent a semi-refusal to Munich regarding Berlin," because "I do not want to kneel in muck." The Berlin party membership did not relent. He met with the regional leadership in September. Apparently, the last obstacle to his accepting the position was his salary. The Gau, which was on the verge of bankruptcy, simply could not afford to pay what Goebbels demanded. National headquarters removed this last barrier by agreeing to pay his salary. This final impediment removed, Goebbels accepted the position.[11]

This appointment indicates several things about the attitudes of the national leadership of the NSDAP. First, the naming of one of the movement's rising stars to the Gauleiter post of Berlin—even going so far as to pay his salary—evinces the seriousness of the Nazis' intent to build a bridgehead in northern Germany, where they had had little success. The NSDAP received a scant 2 percent of Berlin's votes in the most recent Reichstag election. Hitler and his cohorts hoped to improve upon these results. Also, the fact that Goebbels was known for his "leftist" sympathies, which would enable him to appeal to antibourgeois elements in Berlin, indicated the seriousness with which the Nazis intended to pursue the "urban plan," under which they attempted to compete with the proletarian parties (Communists and Socialists) for the support of Germany's workers. Hitler realized that if he were to gain power legally he would need support in northern Germany, and Goebbels would lead the Fuehrer's struggle in the capital city. Berlin had gained a new importance in the movement's plans. It is small wonder that the Berlin party, at least officially, welcomed the news of Goebbels's appointment.[12]

The new Gauleiter assumed leadership of Berlin's three thousand Nazis in November 1926. Among the first things he did was visit the district headquarters in the basement of a *Hinterhaus* on Potsdamerstrasse dubbed the Opiumhoehle (Opium Den). The situation there discouraged him. Permeated by tobacco smoke, the Opium Den was little more than a filthy hangout for unemployed members of the SA. It contained few of the amenities necessary for a serious political party, such as even rudimentary office equipment. Hence, in his first circular to the party membership, Goebbels made acquiring new offices his top priority. It would not be until January 1927 that the Gau moved its headquarters to Lutzowstrasse 44. In the meantime, the new Gau leader informed the party that loitering in the Potsdamerstrasse offices would not be tolerated; it interfered with serious work.[13]

As part of the incentive to get him to go to Berlin, the Fuehrer granted Goebbels powers that no other Gauleiter, with the exception of Hitler himself (Gauleiter of Munich), possessed. Not only could he appoint local leaders, a right traditionally held by the national organization, but Goebbels also controlled the Berlin SA. Instead of reporting to the national SA leadership, Daluege, as chief of the Berlin SA, was responsible directly to the Gau leader. Goebbels realized that, given the history of Gau Berlin, claiming these powers would prove problematic. He was, however, determined to do so. He began this process at a 9 November meeting in the Kriegervereinhaus in Spandau, a stronghold of the movement. As leader of the party in the Reich capital, Goebbels called for an end to all disagreements within the party—they had often led to physical confrontations in the past—and demanded the establishment of unity around his leadership. He insisted that those who rejected these conditions should resign their memberships. One-fifth of the approximately one thousand people present did so. While Goebbels alienated a significant portion of the party membership by his actions, those who remained within the Nazi fold agreed to support him, thereby solidifying his power.[14]

Goebbels also realized that the creation of a strong infrastructure was necessary for his and the party's success and brought order to the previously disorganized Berlin party apparatus. Maintaining that "first the organization had to be strengthened from within, then we could take the struggle for Berlin to the streets," he purged incompetent party leaders. Realizing that the rank and file needed to become more involved in party affairs, he insisted that small assemblies be held, at least weekly, on the local level. Here the conversation was to revolve less around the daily problems of the membership and turn to propagating the Nazi world view. While this caused many apathetic Nazis to resign their memberships, a strong core of dedicated members remained around which Goebbels could construct the party. Larger assemblies of between 1,000 and 1,500 members, usually held in the Kriegervereinhaus, allowed him to deliver his message to the rank and file personally. Weekly meetings, known as *Gautage* (district assemblies), held on Sunday afternoons, brought the leadership of the SA and party organizations together to discuss ideology and propaganda and generally to instill a sense of "direction."[15]

The new Gauleiter also got the party's finances in order, making a special appeal to the membership, which assured him the 1,500 Reichsmarks (RM) per month needed to rent a new headquarters. He also established the Nationalsozialistischer Freiheitsbund (National Socialist Freedom Union). Membership in this exclusive organization came with a special monthly contribution. In four months Goebbels had made the party solvent. The Gau could afford the new headquarters on Luetzowstrasse and had secured 8,000-10,000 RM worth of office equipment as well as an automobile. Fiscal success, coupled with organizational restructuring, made the Berlin NSDAP a well-organized, tightly-knit political organization.[16]

These improvements were but a means to an end: political power. Goebbels held that "whoever conquers the streets, conquers the masses, thereby conquering the state." With this conception of the path to political power, the Nazi leader naturally needed a method for winning the streets, which he saw as dominated by the "Jewish-Bolshevik" hordes of the KPD and Social Democrats (SPD). He would need front-line troops in this struggle, men to fight his battles, and the Berlin SA would provide them. Therefore, Goebbels also reorganized the storm troops on more centralized, hierarchical, lines, assuring his control in the offensive against "Red Berlin."[17]

The Gauleiter's view of the struggle for the streets was different from the traditional rabble-rousing, nihilistic violence characteristic of the Berlin SA before his arrival. Violent clashes with the Communist or Socialist paramilitary organizations, the Red Front Fighters' League (RFB) and the Reichsbanner respectively, would no longer be the *raison d'etre* of the SA. In accordance with Hitler's plans to make the NSDAP a legitimate political party, it would become more of a propaganda troop. The storm trooper's primary goal was to become representative of the Nazi Party, to make it visible to the masses, to serve as "the vanguard of the movement." He would not only physically turn back the "Reds" but also march in *Aufmaersche* (parades) and distribute flyers. The SA should establish, Goebbels argued, that the NSDAP was willing to fight for Germany's honor, that the Nazis were a party, not of words like all the rest, but of deeds, of action. Hence, although the barroom brawls with the enemy that the SA men so enjoyed were necessary, they should not be ends in themselves. In order to mold the SA into what Goebbels wanted it to be, discipline had to be imposed; the SA needed to behave like a real army.[18]

These concepts would serve the Nazi leader well in the long run, during the six-year struggle for power in the streets of Berlin. They were also important to his immediate concern. The biggest problem facing the Berlin NSDAP was the simple fact that it was largely ignored. It was but one of numerous right-wing fringe groups within the city; many Berliners had not even heard of it. What the Nazis of Berlin needed above all else was publicity; they needed to be noticed. Goebbels, holding that "Berlin needs sensation like a fish needs water," was prepared to provide it to gain the attention of the citizens of the city. If he caused enough large disturbances, he believed that even Berliners, largely anesthetized by all the political activity in the Reich capital, would notice. Propaganda, including political violence, would be his means of achieving this goal.[19]

An excellent way to promote violent reaction to his party's activities was to take the fight to the enemy's territory, to take the political offensive. Hence, many Nazi *Massenversammlungen* (mass rallies) took place in working-class districts of Berlin. This not only would serve to foment confrontation with the "Reds" but would also take the Nazi message directly to its target, the proletariat, especially those who had been deceived into supporting Marxism.[20]

The offensive began soon after Goebbels arrived in the city. On 14 November 1926, Berlin's 280 SA men marched "through the red stronghold of Neukoelln." Onlookers had assaulted many of the Nazis on their way to the assembly point for the march, and, so the Nazi account goes, members of the RFB lined the parade route along the Kaiser-Friedrich Strasse, singing the "Internationale." The RFB, wielding knives, allegedly physically assaulted the peaceful marchers as well. In spite of being attacked on the Hermannplatz, the SA continued to its goal, Hallesches Tor. Thirteen storm troopers were badly hurt, but the march was a success. The SA men had paraded through a working-class district, establishing that the Communists did not control the streets and gaining much-needed publicity.[21]

Minor actions such as the parade through Neukoelln continued, but it was not until 25 January 1927 that Goebbels scored his first major propaganda success. On that day, he held a mass rally at the Seitz Festsaele in Spandau. Five hundred RFB men were in attendance, hoping to disturb the assembly. The Nazis, Goebbels later claimed, were interested in an honest debate, so the SA expelled all troublemakers. The two-hour meeting was a straightforward attempt to win the proletariat from Marxism, he argued, to speak "man to man." Violence erupted when, as a member of the RFB took the podium to rebut Goebbels, the Gau leader conveniently received word that Communists had assaulted two Nazis who had left the meeting early. One of them had been stabbed and supposedly lay dying in the hospital. The Gauleiter announced that he would not carry on a discussion with murderers, and the Communist approaching the podium shoved him away from it. Seeing their leader assaulted, the SA attacked the RFB. A brawl ensued, during which the outnumbered Communists retreated. The SA remained in control of the hall and had, Goebbels held, achieved an important moral victory.[22]

An even more dramatic clash took place about three weeks later in the Pharussaele, a popular location for KPD assemblies in the proletarian district of Wedding. The posters announcing a Nazi meeting to take place there proclaimed that "The bourgeois state is approaching its end. A new Germany must be forged. Workers of the brain and fist, in your hands lies the destiny of the German people. On Friday, 11 February, Pharussaele! Theme: the break-up of the bourgeois class state." The poster is evidence of a popular Nazi propaganda ploy: emphasizing National Socialism's sympathy for the working class and hatred of capitalism. It did not work, however. The RFB placed stickers outside of the Pharussaele stating: "Red Wedding for the Red proletariat. Whoever dares to put his foot into the Pharus-Saele will be beaten to a pulp."[23]

Goebbels, the featured speaker for the evening, arrived in Wedding at about 8:00 P.M. to discover Communists roaming the streets waiting to harass Nazis on their way to the rally. Upon reaching the door of the hall, the Gauleiter's story goes, the leader of the SS (Schutzstaffel or bodyguard) guard informed him that the police had closed the doors at 7:15 and that a full two-thirds of the two thousand spectators present were Communists. Goebbels saw an opportunity to reach the proletarian masses and expose the lies their Marxist leaders had spread about the NSDAP, so he decided to give his speech before the hostile audience. As he approached the podium, cries of *"Bluthund"* (bloodhound) and *"Arbeitermoerder"* (murderer of workers) filled the hall. The crowd would not be quieted. Fifteen SA and SS men surrounded the stage as Goebbels tried to speak. Each time he began, a Communist in the rear of the hall shouted, "Point of order!" The assembly leader, Daluege, informed the heckler that, since this was a Nazi meeting, he had no right to bring up a point of order. Goebbels dispatched his guards to quiet down the troublemaker, whom the storm troopers carried to the stage.[24]

At this point, someone threw a beer glass at the podium. A pitched battle resulted. Glasses, beer bottles, table legs, and chairs served as weapons. The Nazis were able to drive out their opponents, making Goebbels's claims that the assembly was two-thirds Communist appear doubtful. Daluege then called the meeting to order, and Goebbels gave one of the most important speeches he would make during the "time of struggle." He had ten of the most seriously injured storm troopers brought up on the stage. There, surrounded by bleeding "aristocrats of the Third Reich," he ended his speech with exhortations to the "unknown SA man," who fought not for self-aggrandizement but for the glorification of Germany. The Gau leader had developed a powerful new propaganda motif to which he would often turn during the next six years. By the time the meeting ended, the police had cleared the streets outside the hall, thereby avoiding further violence.[25]

That was not the end of the matter. The Berlin Nazis received a further windfall from the battle in the Pharussaele: publicity. The major Berlin papers carried stories about the incident, which Goebbels quoted at length in his own account. The *Berliner Morgenpost* counted fourteen injured in the brawl, four of whom had to be hospitalized. The newspaper insisted, in a more credible estimate than that of the Nazis, that one hundred Communists were present. The *Welt am Abend* claimed that Daluege said that there would be no open discussion as promised and that three hundred men attacked the justifiably angry Communists who protested this development.[26]

The confrontation received front-page coverage in the Communist daily, *Rote Fahne*. The Communist paper claimed, like the *Welt am Abend*, that the Nazis denied the Communists present the opportunity to voice their opinions. Then, this account continues, the Nazis attacked the workers present without provocation. The workers, caught off guard because of their peaceful intentions, were the unsuspecting and undeserving victims of Nazi thugs wielding table legs and chairs.[27]

Probably neither the account of the Communists nor that of the Nazis was entirely accurate. Exactly what occurred in the Pharussaele will never be known. Much more important, however, from the point of view of the historian, were the results. The NSDAP gained valuable publicity; people talked about the party. A political movement consisting of a few thousand adherents had become a force in the capital city. Berliners simply could no longer ignore the Nazis.

The newly won political notoriety of the Berlin Nazi Party led to an increase in the number of violent clashes between the SA and RFB. Among the most interesting of these episodes occurred in March in the Lichterfelde-Ost train station. Members of the SA were returning from a ceremony in the town of Trebbin. RFB men were on the same train, also returning from a rally, theirs in Leuna. According to Nazi accounts, when the train halted in Lichterfelde, in the southern reaches of Berlin, the RFB fired upon the detrained Nazis as the train rolled out of the station. In response, a storm trooper jumped upon the train and pulled the emergency brake. A fight ensued in which the SS troops awaiting the arrival of their comrades became involved. Between sixty and one hundred shots were fired. At least two storm troopers were hit, one in the leg and the other in the pelvis.[28]

The police intervened and, Goebbels recounted, escorted the defeated RFB from the station. Fifteen Communists were hurt. The Nazis assembled outside the station and marched north to the Kurfuerstendamm, the cultural center of Berlin. Once there, they assaulted Jewish passersby on the street, and were even so bold as to enter the Romanische Cafe, a salon at the center of Berlin's intellectual life, in pursuit of Jews.[29]

This incident earned the Nazis much publicity; the story even occupied the first two pages of *Rote Fahne*. It recounts, in a version somewhat different from Goebbels's, how four to five hundred Nazis fired upon "20-25 Communist workers" without provocation. The SA and SS, not the RFB, had guns. In the bloody battle that ensued, the Nazis inflicted wounds upon twenty Communists, six of whom were badly hurt, while suffering a mere two injuries themselves. *Rote Fahne* as much as admitted that the "fascists" won this battle when it said that "when, in the future, bands of fascists attack workers, events must not proceed as in Lichterfelde," but the Nazis must feel the "fist" of the proletariat.[30]

Goebbels, while realizing that political violence could help gain a reputation as a dynamic movement for the NSDAP, also knew that it could get the party into serious trouble. Therefore, at the beginning of 1927, he issued orders forbidding the SA to carry weapons, hopefully avoiding another prohibition as in 1923. This order did not prevent the storm troopers from arming themselves, however, and, in the long run, the much-feared prohibition came. When it did, the possession of weapons was not an issue.[31]

Events reached their climax after Hitler gave a speech exclusively to party members—he was forbidden to give public speeches in Prussia—in a Berlin beer hall called the "Clou" on 1 May 1927. Because of a negative reaction to the speech in the "Jewish" press, Goebbels called a public assembly to rebut newspaper accounts of the Fuehrer's address. This meeting in the Kriegervereinhaus on 4 May would have a dramatic impact upon the fortunes of National Socialism in Berlin.[32]

According to Goebbels, the assembly was full and the police had to deny many people admittance. He began his speech with an attack upon the "Jewish" press of Berlin, which had published a fabricated interview with Hitler, misrepresenting his ideas. During the address, a drunk in the right-center of the hall interrupted the Gauleiter. The audience allegedly became angry with the man, and in order to avoid chaos, Goebbels directed the SA to expel him. After "boxing him on the ears," the storm troopers did so. The speaker thought nothing of the incident—it was not unusual for someone to be forcibly removed from a Nazi rally—and continued his presentation.[33]

Then a police officer stood on a chair, attempting to make an announcement. Goebbels, the Gauleiter claimed in his memoirs, quieted down the crowd so that it could hear the officer, who informed those present that they would be searched for weapons. The Nazi leader ordered them to submit. It took around two hours to search the audience of two to three thousand. To this point, nothing had occurred out of the ordinary, and Goebbels had no reason to anticipate subsequent events.[34]

The following morning Goebbels was distressed to discover that the Berlin press, because of events on the previous evening, was mounting a campaign to have his party prohibited. It seems that the "provocateur" was a Lutheran minister. The papers, seizing upon the opportunity to discredit the Nazis, recounted a "serious assault" with a beer mug, not a "boxing on the ears." The "Jewish" press, Goebbels claimed, called the two storm troopers involved "murderers" and said that the victim had to be taken to the hospital.[35]

From the point of view of the Nazis, things only got worse. Around seven in the evening, a policeman arrived at party headquarters to inform them that the president of the Berlin Police Force, Karl Zoergiebel, had issued a prohibition against the NSDAP. The grounds given for the ban cited "around 30" incidents since October 1926 in which the Nazis had attacked bystanders and "members of opposing organizations." The National Socialists, under the terms of the prohibition, might not hold "assemblies of any kind," including those in private. "Parades and demonstrations" were also expressly banned.[36]

The immediate response of the Nazis was to send a storm trooper to Zoergiebel's office. He returned the notification of the ban to the office, shouting, "We National Socialists refuse to recognize the prohibition." Goebbels, however, realizing the gravity of the situation, composed a letter to the Prussian Minister of the Interior, Albert Grzenski, protesting the ban.

It was illegal for two reasons, the Gauleiter contended. First, the Gau Gross-Berlin included all of the Mark Brandenburg. Authorities of the city of Berlin could not prohibit an organization that was, for the most part, outside of their jurisdiction. Second, the prohibition was politically motivated. Clearly, the police wanted to muzzle a group so critical of the system. The KPD had clearly committed much worse indiscretions, Goebbels continued, and the police had not prohibited the Communists. The Gauleiter concluded his letter by declaring that the movement would never be vanquished.[37]

This last statement proved prophetic. The NSDAP did not dissolve but went underground. Numerous Nazi groups reorganized under different guises. Some became "stamp collecting clubs," others "hiking" or "sports clubs." Yet others became "singing" or "bowling" groups. Some even went so far as to dub themselves "Bible-study" groups. All this served to add credence to the slogan of these dark days for the NSDAP, "Trotz Verbot nicht tot!" ("Not dead in spite of prohibition!").[38]

The ban, however, hurt the Nazis severely. The police kept a close eye upon the forbidden party, and it could no longer operate in the open. Although the ban was not extended outside of the Reich capital, and meetings could be held in Potsdam, it proved impossible to carry out propaganda activities. (Goebbels was partially correct in claiming that Berlin authorities could not prohibit an organization with members outside of their jurisdiction, but while Berlin authorities could not extend the *Verbot* outside the city, they could prosecute it within Berlin.) The SA could no longer march into Communist strongholds. To complicate matters further, soon after the ban on the party, authorities placed a *Redeverbot* (prohibition on public speaking) upon Goebbels, thereby completing the silencing of the Nazis. The Gauleiter realized that, without an effective propaganda apparatus, the party might well fade into oblivion, as had happened during previous bans. Goebbels needed to find another means of propagating his hateful message. Further, he wanted to continue to garner the publicity that his often violent antics had gained for the NSDAP. The Gauleiter decided to start a weekly newspaper.[39]

2

An Institutional History of *Der Angriff* 1927-1933

The establishment of a newspaper as a means of spreading Nazi propaganda in Berlin, although not a novel idea, gained a new urgency in the spring of 1927. Julius Lippert, *Chef der Geschaeftstelle* (chief of party headquarters) and later editor-in-chief of *Der Angriff* (*The Attack*), recounted a meeting of the Gau leadership soon after the police outlawed the party. At the gathering held in the Gauleiter's apartment, Goebbels developed the idea of publishing a weekly newspaper. This would not violate the terms of the prohibition. In addition to permitting the Berlin Nazis to continue their propaganda activities, the office of a weekly publication would serve as a structure that would keep the outlawed party intact. This last function was probably most attractive to the Gau leadership, for the prohibition was a serious threat to the NSDAP's existence.[1]

Goebbels also decided, after much discussion, upon the name of the new weekly. Realizing that the title of his newspaper would be very important in attracting readers, he held that it should both "agitate" and present the paper's program. The name decided upon, *The Attack*, indicated that the purpose of the publication was to "take the offensive." It was, contended Lippert, a "meaningful [and] powerful" title for a *Kampfzeitschrift* ("fighting periodical").[2]

The type of organ that the Berlin Gau leadership hoped to create, a *Kampfblatt* or *Kampfzeitung* ("fighting newspaper"), evolved from the long tradition of the German political press. The revolutions of 1848 saw the development of newspapers

affiliated with political parties. The second half of the nine-
teenth century witnessed the creation of the most influential
political newspapers, the Catholic Center Party's *Germania*
and the SPD's *Vorwaerts*. The *raison d'etre* of these political
organs was not the spread of information as much as the
spread of the party program.[3]

As was the case in so many other areas, the revolution of
1918 led to a radicalization of the German political press. The
Communist Party's *Rote Fahne* took polemical attacks upon
its opponents to new extremes, and its political enemies answered in kind. In the milieu of the first years of the Weimar
Republic, the political press gained increasing influence, leading to a rise in the number of politically affiliated newspapers.[4]

The political right also improved and expanded its press,
and the Nazis were among the first *voelkisch* groups to develop
a press apparatus. In December 1920, Hitler bought the insolvent *Voelkischer Beobachter*, making it the first Nazi newspaper. Its primary functions were to communicate the official
party line to the membership and serve as a source of information concerning meetings and other party activities. Local
Nazi leaders, emulating their Fuehrer, founded their own papers. The most pressing reason for founding these organs was
to enhance the local propaganda apparatus; to have yet one
more tool in the battle with the system. A newspaper also
served as an organizational tool around which the party could
be built.[5]

The political press reflected the ever more prevalent violence characteristic of the Weimar years. The "fighting press"
was characterized by sensationalism, an unrelenting partisanship, emphasis upon violent clashes with the "enemy," an
almost complete disregard for hard news, and a concentration
upon polemic. A fighting newspaper was not a source of information; it related a savage nihilism that would appeal to the
dispossessed of Weimar Germany. The Nazis and Communists
proved the most effective political factions at producing these
newspapers. Goebbels hoped *Der Angriff* would be such a
journal.[6]

Before he could begin publishing his newspaper Goebbels

had to overcome several obstacles, the most important of which was political in nature. Goebbels's relationship with the Strassers, which had been somewhat cool since his change in allegiance during the summer of 1926, became more strained. In May 1927, in order to avoid alienating Hitler, who was feuding with the Strassers, Goebbels resigned his editorship of the Kampfverlag's *NS-Briefe*, a position he had held since the periodical's inception in 1925. When rumors of a split between the Gauleiter and Hitler began to circulate in the "bourgeois" press, Goebbels blamed the Strassers. In order to discredit such rumors, he began to attack the brothers viciously, insisting that the Reichsleitung discipline them or accept his resignation from the Gau leadership post.[7]

The rift between Goebbels and the Strasser camp widened. The Berlin Gauleiter attacked Gregor Strasser in retaliation for an article that appeared in the Kampfverlag's seven newspapers in April 1927. Entitled "Consequences of Race Mixture," Goebbels alleged that it was an attack upon him personally because of its references to a clubfoot. Although signed by an Elberfeld Nazi, Erich Koch, Goebbels insisted that Gregor Strasser had written it as part of a systematic press campaign against the Berlin leadership. On 10 June, sixteen leaders of the Berlin branch of the party met at the behest of their leader. He demanded that they renew their pledge of loyalty to him and went on to harangue the absent Strassers for the newspaper article. Although Koch swore that he had indeed written the article himself and did not have Goebbels in mind when composing it, the disagreement escalated.[8]

The Strassers pursued a vigorous counterattack against Goebbels, centering it upon his proposed newspaper. The Kampfverlag already published a newspaper in Berlin, the official Gau organ, the *Berliner Arbeiter Zeitung* or *BAZ*. Gregor Strasser saw *Der Angriff* as a serious threat to the *BAZ*, insisting that Hitler stop publication of the new paper. The Fuehrer compromised, decreeing that *Der Angriff* be "neutral," meaning that it would not be the official party organ. Although recognized by the party, it was to be the Gauleiter's personal press outlet, not a tool of the party as such. Strasser's protestations that, given his position, Goebbels could never be considered editor of a "neutral" paper fell on deaf ears.[9]

The Fuehrer's solution to the disagreement concerning the newspapers set the tone for the way in which he settled the Goebbels-Strasser dispute. The Gau leader was Hitler's personal representative in Berlin, so he had to side with him in the long term. On the other hand, the Nazi "left" had an extensive following in the movement, and breaking with the Strassers would be counterproductive. In addition, a continuation of the status quo would be to Hitler's advantage because it would preclude an alliance of the two factions in a region where his power was tentative. Hitler's solution was to publish an article in the *Voelkischer Beobachter* stating that reports of his falling-out with Goebbels published in the *Berliner Tageblatt*, the *Vossische Zeitung*, and the *Welt am Abend* were false. Jews, determined to weaken Nazism, had fomented these stories. Indeed, Goebbels maintained Hitler's "fullest loyalty." The Fuehrer permitted publication of *Der Angriff* on schedule and had publicly announced his support for the Gauleiter, giving Goebbels a major victory. In the long run, however, the disagreement remained unresolved and the fight between Goebbels and the Strassers would continue until 1930. *Der Angriff* would play an important role in this ongoing dispute.[10]

While carrying out a public argument with the Strassers, Goebbels also began to prepare for the coming publication of *Der Angriff*. Among the first things he did was secure the funds necessary to finance the enterprise. He borrowed 2,000 RM from a still unknown source and found a printer willing to extend credit. Lippert played an important role in convincing Hans Schulze, a local printer and member of the NSDAP, to undertake such an economically dubious enterprise. The greatest obstacle to the founding of a newspaper—acquiring the necessary capital—was overcome.[11]

A vigorous propaganda campaign designed to publicize the upcoming first edition of *Der Angriff* began in June 1927. Goebbels issued a series of three posters anticipating its publication. The first, clearly designed to pique the curiosity of the reader, asked simply "THE ATTACK?" The second announced that "The Attack begins on 4 July;" and the third informed the reader that *Der Angriff* would be "the German Monday paper." The newspaper, this last poster announced, would be published by Goebbels and have as its motto, "Fuer die Unterdrueckten! Gegen die Ausbeuter!" (For the Oppressed! Against the Exploiters!).[12]

Perhaps the most important requisite for founding a newspaper was the assembly of a competent staff. Goebbels would himself serve as *Herausgeber* (publisher) and oversee the overall operation of *Der Angriff*, especially when it came to determining its ideological line. He had experience in publishing a periodical (*NS-Briefe*); finding others qualified in the field of journalism, however, would prove problematic. There were not many Berlin Nazis with experience in this area. Since Goebbels hoped to maintain the organization of the now illegal Gau offices, many party administrators simply assumed new positions on the staff of *Der Angriff*; this only served to intensify the problem. This largely unqualified press organization faced the formidable task of founding a new paper. Goebbels's difficulties were far from over.[13]

Goebbels chose as *Hauptschriftleiter* (editor-in-chief), the man who would oversee the daily operation of the newspaper, Julius Lippert, one of the few men available with experience in journalism. In addition to having served as chief of the Berlin party's information office and giving speeches relating Nazi views on economic matters, Lippert had published several articles in the *voelkisch* press. Born in Basel in 1895, he had a doctorate from the University of Berlin. He had joined the party officially only three months before the publication of the first issue of the paper, but probably had been sympathetic to the NSDAP for some time. After the "seizure of power," he went on to become *Staatskommissar* (mayor) of Berlin.[14]

As editor-in-chief, Lippert was in charge of the daily operation of *Der Angriff*, a task for which Goebbels had neither the patience nor the inclination. The Gauleiter simply did not wish to endure the tedium inherent in a regular job; he had other responsibilities. Lippert was a convenient tool who would see to the more mundane aspects of journalism without posing a serious threat to the publisher's authority. Lippert often acted as an intermediary between Goebbels and *Der Angriff's* staff. For example, he carried out the Gauleiter's orders to discipline employees of the paper. The editor-in-chief also served as a convenient scapegoat when Goebbels was displeased with the paper's copy. He simply blamed any deficiencies upon Lippert's "bourgeois" world view, often haranguing the editor-in-chief on this score, insisting that *Der Angriff* must become more *voelkisch* and "socialist." In spite of this conflict, Lippert evidently did an adequate job, also serving as editor for foreign politics from 1930 to 1933. The Gauleiter decided to offer Lippert the position of editor-in-chief when *Der Angriff* became a daily in 1930.[15]

Dagobert Duerr assisted Lippert in overseeing the paper's staff. Born in 1897 in Mecklenburg, Duerr joined the NSDAP in 1925 and became chief of the Berlin party office (*Gaugeschaeftsfuehrer*) in January 1927. Like so many other leaders of the now illegal Berlin Nazi party, Duerr went to work for *Der Angriff* in July 1927. What his official title was is somewhat uncertain; the sources list several, and it is possible that he went by all of them at various times. The official party archive lists him as *Chef vom Dienst* (head of the newspaper's office) for the years 1927-1931, but he called himself *Stellvertretender Hauptschriftleiter* (deputy editor-in-chief) in his personnel records. In 1932, he became editor for domestic politics, which meant that he, like Lippert, wrote much of the newspaper. The practice of one man filling multiple posts was probably a device designed to save money, which was always in short supply. After the Nazis assumed power, Duerr became press chief of Berlin.[16]

Although Goebbels, Lippert, and Duerr dominated the operation of *Der Angriff* throughout the "years of struggle," several other people played significant roles in the paper's operation, the most intriguing of these being Hans Schweitzer, who drew the political cartoons for the paper. Born in 1901 in Berlin, he became a member of the party in 1926. Even before he joined the staff of *Der Angriff*, he was famous in Berlin as an illustrator of political posters and postcards. As Goebbels put it, "Schweitzer is a fabulous illustrator. He has the great gift of being able to make a vital point with a few lines. Only a master can do that." Schweitzer became the Gauleiter's closest companion during the Weimar years; they regularly spent the evenings together, attending the movies or the theater. Goebbels, who considered himself a writer, probably enjoyed the companionship of someone with an artistic temperament. In 1928 they jointly published the infamous *Das Buch Isidor*, a vicious polemic against the vice president of the Berlin police, Bernhard Weiss. Schweitzer published his caricatures under the pseudonym "Mjoelnir," the name of the hammer possessed by the god Donner in Wagner's "Ring Cycle." Mjoelnir's caricatures were brilliant, and, as Goebbels pointed out, it was often easier to express Nazi ideas in a political cartoon than with the written word. A cartoon would express concepts in a quickly understood manner that was impossible to attain in an article. During the Third Reich, Schweitzer rose to the rank of colonel in the SS and became a Reich senator of culture.[17]

Schweitzer's style was indicative of the overall tone of *Der Angriff*. He emphasized simplicity and the brutality of life on the streets of the German capital. This is in sharp contrast to the style of other Nazi cartoonists, such as "Fips" (Philip Ruprecht), who worked for Juilius Streicher's infamous newspaper, *Der Stuermer*. Whereas Fips emphasized miscegenation—a typical cartoon in *Der Stuermer* would show a hooknosed Jew deflowering a defenseless Aryan girl—the theme of Mjoelnir's cartoons was usually either economics or political violence. This variation is reflective not only of the differing tastes of their respective publishers but also of the audiences at whom the two newspapers were aimed. *Der Stuermer* mirrors the obsession with sexuality so typical of the uneducated farmers who read the paper. Goebbels, on the other hand, considered *Der Angriff* a working-class newspaper. Schweitzer's cartoons reflected this fact. Indeed, Mjoelnir's style had more in common with that of the Communist cartoonists working for *Rote Fahne* than it had with Fips's. This is evidence of the fact that regional party leaders had a great deal of latitude in devising their own propaganda motifs, which were determined, to a large extent, by local conditions. One thing that the work of Fips and Mjoelnir had in common, however, was a vicious anti-Semitism. It can be said that anti-Semitism was characteristic of *all* Nazi propaganda. *Der Angriff* was no exception to this trend.[18]

Eberhard Assmann, erstwhile chief of the Gau's economic department, became managing editor of *Der Angriff*. Born in 1903, he joined the party in 1925. His job was to oversee the actual printing and publication of *Der Angriff*. In November 1930, Ludwig Weissauer, who also served as editor for economics, replaced him. Goebbels expelled Weissauer in 1931 because of his role in a failed SA rebellion.[19]

Weissauer's replacement, Hans Hinkel, was born in Worms in 1901. After studying at the Universities of Bonn and Munich, he joined the NSDAP in October 1921. In 1924, Hinkel became editor-in-chief of the *Oberbayrischen Tageszeitung*, a Nazi newspaper. In 1928, he went to work for the Kampfverlag, which caused him to move to Berlin. While in the German capital, he became a correspondent for the *Voelkischer Beobachter* and, after the Stennes Putsch, managing editor of *Der Angriff*. Because of his extensive experience in journalism, Hinkel became an important member of the staff, writing much of the newspaper's copy. He was also secretary of the Kampfbund fuer deutsche Kultur, the Nazi organization which attempted to eliminate "Jewish" (modernist) culture, a position that took up much of his time. Therefore, although he was among the most capable members of *Der Angriff's* staff, Hinkel's authority at the newspaper never reached its potential. After the Nazis came to power, Hinkel worked his way up the party apparatus, becoming a *Staatskommissar* in the Prussian Ministry of Sciences, Art and Popular Education, as well as member of the Prussian Theater Committee.[20]

Another member of *Der Angriff's* staff is of interest because she was a woman in a man's world. Melitta Wiedemann must have been a person of extraordinary talent to have risen to a position of responsibility in the patriarchal hierarchy of National Socialism. She served as secretary in the offices of *Der Angriff* and in 1929 assumed an editor's position on the newspaper, overseeing women's issues until 1931. At first, Goebbels had a rather high opinion of her abilities, calling her "the only real man" on the editorial staff. In the long run, however, she was in an impossible position. Other members of the staff were jealous of her abilities, and she became a victim of Nazi misogyny. In the end, Goebbels changed his mind about her, confessing that he did "not trust Wiedemann," because "a woman will always misuse power." The Gauleiter's chauvinism was probably the real reason for her expulsion from the party after the Stennes Putsch; at the time of the SA rebellion she was out of the country and hence clearly not directly involved.[21]

There were others, like Wiedemann, Weissauer, and Hinkel, who joined the editorial staff of *Der Angriff* at some time after the inception of the newspaper. Willi Krause, a Berliner born in 1907, had joined the NSDAP in August 1930. He had served as an editor for Scherl-Verlag, bringing with him valuable experience to the position of editor for local politics, a post he assumed in the fall of 1930. Later he was editor for cultural politics. Like the other editors of the newspaper, he wrote much of the copy himself, making film reviews his specialty. After serving *Der Angriff* for the remainder of the *Kampfzeit*, he became a film critic for the Propaganda Ministry.[22]

Karoly Kampmann was a latecomer to the newspaper's editorial staff. Having joined the party in 1930, he worked his way up the hierarchy of the SA, becoming *Gaupropagandaleiter* of Berlin in August 1931. In January 1933, Kampmann replaced Lippert as editor-in-chief of *Der Angriff*. Although Goebbels never explicitly stated why he fired Lippert, the Gauleiter's diaries make it clear that the two had had another clash concerning the ideological line of the organ, and Goebbels decided to remove his second in command. His replacement, who went on to work as press chief for the Reich labor leader, had little direct effect upon *Der Angriff* during the years 1927-1933.[23]

While the editorial staff composed most of the articles in

the newspaper, there were other journalists who regularly wrote for *Der Angriff* as well as other organs of the far right. Known as *Mitarbeiter* (associates), these people were freelance writers paid by the line of copy. Although there is little evidence concerning the role of these journalists in the publication of Goebbels's newspaper, it is clear that they wrote most of the relatively few signed articles in *Der Angriff*. Among the most interesting of these writers was Johann von Leers. Born in Mecklenburg in 1902, von Leers had a doctorate. Like many unemployed intellectuals during the Weimar Republic, he became active in *voelkisch* politics, joining first the Free Corps Viking and, in 1929, the Nazi Party. After supporting himself as a freelance writer through articles published in the NSDAP press, von Leers joined the SS and became an important author in the Reich Propaganda Ministry, publishing such books as *Kraefte hinter Roosevelt* and *14 Jahre Judenrepublik*. Like so many other employees of *Der Angriff*, von Leers used his position as a stepping-stone to higher positions in the Third Reich.[24]

The leaders at the offices of *Der Angriff* shared several traits. They were well-educated, all having college degrees, several of them doctorates. They were young, middle-class people who had no place in the Weimar system and felt alienated by a society coming increasingly under the influence of working-class institutions. All but one was male, and most had become Nazis relatively recently. These characteristics imply that ideological purity was not as important as competence to Goebbels; he hired people who could complete the tasks assigned to them. That they be orthodox Nazis was not his primary concern. As Gauleiter and publisher he, not the editorial staff, would oversee the ideological purity of the paper.

Even before the appearance of the first issue, *Der Angriff* began fulfilling one of its two major goals: its offices provided an opportunity to maintain the illegal party organization. Goebbels gave most of the former leaders of Gau Gross-Berlin positions in Angriff-Verlag. Dozens of storm troopers, who might otherwise have drifted away from the defunct party, volunteered to work for the weekly, both in the writing and publishing of the newspaper as well as distribution. The newspaper distribution firm Stilke oversaw sales of the paper. SA men sold the newspaper on street corners as did newspaper stands owned by Nazis on Potsdamer Platz and Alexanderplatz. *Der Angriff* was also available at certain bookstores and newspaper stands outside of Berlin.[25]

Although the almost complete lack of journalistic experience surely diminished the quality of *Der Angriff*, in addition to causing severe difficulties in getting it out on time, the party leadership considered the paper a success. A hard core of party members thought of the weekly as their own and worked hard at the offices of the paper. These same people who created *Der Angriff*, and persevered through the lean years of Nazism in the capital city, were rewarded when the NSDAP became a dynamic political force after 1930 and assumed power in January 1933. *Der Angriff* helped to hold the party together in difficult times.[26]

The first issue of *Der Angriff* appeared on 4 July 1927. It was a disappointment to its publisher, who considered it a *Kaeseblatt* (paper for wrapping cheese—a popular slang term for an unimportant, uninteresting journal). Although Goebbels considered the weekly uninspiring, he had to continue its publication since it was his only means of communicating with the membership. The quality of the paper improved over time, as the staff members became increasingly competent at their jobs; but this was a protracted process, and the newspaper would never consistently meet Goebbels's standards.[27]

The 4 July edition of *Der Angriff* was laid out as it would be, for the most part, for the remainder of the Weimar era. In addition to the title of the paper, the masthead contained its motto: in the upper left-hand corner "For the Oppressed," and in the right "Against the Exploiters." To the left, under the title, were the words: "Publisher: Dr. Goebbels." Directly under the title was "The German Monday Paper in Berlin." The price of the first issue, which would remain constant until the paper became a daily in 1930, was twenty pfennigs. Noticeably absent from the masthead, which would remain almost unchanged during the *Kampfzeit*, was the official party symbol, the swastika. This was because *Der Angriff*, being technically the private property of the Gauleiter, was not the official Gau organ. That distinction belonged to the Strassers' BAZ. Although recognized by the party as an NSDAP paper, *Der Angriff*, like many other party journals, could not use the swastika. Hitler probably refused permission in order to mollify the Strassers, who had fought against the publication of the newspaper. Even after *Der Angriff* became the official newspaper of Gau Berlin in 1930, the editorial staff never used the party symbol on the masthead.[28]

The lead story in the first issue dealt with the possibility of a Communist putsch, and the political cartoon, also on the first page, intimated that Foreign Minister Gustav Stresemann's policy of fulfillment of the Treaty of Versailles was tantamount to surrendering Germany to the Jews. The second page presented major news stories from a Nazi perspective. The following page contained the "Political Diary." Written, like the lead story, by Goebbels himself, the "Political Diary" was a record of major political events during the week, as interpreted by Berlin's leading Nazi. The second edition of *Der Angriff* printed announcements of local party meetings. Entitled "Plakatsaeule" ("Poster Column"), this listing became a permanent fixture on page three. "Kampf um Berlin" ("Struggle for Berlin"), appearing on page four, related the activities of the local NSDAP, especially violent clashes with other political groups.[29]

The short-lived anti-Semitic section, "Der Philosemit," appeared on the next page. It dealt primarily with the perceived dangers of Jewish influence in German culture and politics. At the bottom of the page, squared-in for emphasis, was the statement, "The Jewish people will never relinquish its goal of eliminating all that is German from the world." The editors of the newspaper, possibly because they realized that a column dedicated solely to anti-Semitism in a newspaper saturated with anti-Jewish polemic was redundant, and that the space could be used more productively, eliminated this section in August 1927. Pages six and eight carried advertisements. As a Nazi newspaper, *Der Angriff* could not accept advertisements from Jewish firms. Most advertisers throughout the "years of struggle" were small and medium-sized companies attempting to sell such things as SA uniforms and cigarettes. Sandwiched between the advertisement pages was the page concerned with local news, "From the Reich Capital."[30]

Eventually another column appeared that concentrated upon Berlin news. "From the Asphalt Desert" referred to the streets of the German capital. The column dealt with events at the grass-roots level, always keeping the NSDAP's program in mind. The first story to appear on this page denied claims that storm troopers had purposely run over a Jew's dog, "Salln." Another column, "Wie sie sich amuesieren" ("How They Amuse Themselves") reviewed theater, film, and radio from a Nazi perspective. *Der Angriff* found Berlin's cultural life lacking in opportunities for the working man, who had "neither money nor time" for the frivolous products of modern culture. Catering to the tastes of Jews and democrats, these productions were unfit for German consumption. The sixteenth of January saw the first appearance of a section presenting the Berlin NSDAP's perspective on economic matters, "Arbeit und Geld" ("Work and Money").[31]

In January 1929, *Der Angriff* first appeared in an edition consisting of twelve pages, allowing the weekly's staff to develop sections with new subjects. Now the newspaper contained a supplement that alternated its theme between women's issues—"Heim und Welt" ("Home and World")—and the SA, "Der unbekannte SA Mann" ("The Unknown SA Man"). In addition, *Der Angriff* began to publish book reviews and a new column presenting a Nazi view of German history, "What History Teaches." This section published highly didactic accounts of historical events designed to show how outside forces—Jews, Marxists and democrats—had conspired to deprive Germany of its rightful place among nations.[32]

On 3 October 1929, *Der Angriff* began appearing twice weekly, Mondays and Thursdays. Although the staff returned the newspaper to an eight-page format, the semiweekly publication schedule permitted the editors to expand the issues dealt with yet again. Two new columns were added, one for the Hitler Youth and another for students ("Students in Brown Shirts"). In May 1930, *Der Angriff* expanded to ten pages, making it possible to publish more advertisements as well as propaganda.[33]

Beginning 1 November 1930, after a protracted negotiation process, *Der Angriff* began daily publication. The editorial staff began discussing the possibility of publishing *Der Angriff* on a daily basis as early as May 1929. Serious obstacles, however, confronted Goebbels's plans. The Gauleiter first broached the subject with Hitler on the second anniversary of the first issue of the paper. The proposal that he made to the Fuehrer involved Hitler becoming publisher of the daily while Goebbels would serve as editor-in chief himself. He hoped to begin publication on the first of January. Goebbels's diary entry does not record his leader's reaction, but, in light of subsequent developments, it is likely that Hitler chose to defer a decision on the issue.[34]

The first important discussion of the possibility of making *Der Angriff* a daily occurred when Goebbels met with Hitler, Max Amann, head of Eher Verlag, the Nazi publishing company based in Munich, and Rudolf Hess, the Fuehrer's secretary. Amann approved of Goebbels's plan but insisted that, in order to make the paper solvent, 40,000 RM had to be raised and eight thousand subscribers found before Goebbels could begin publication. When the National Socialist Women's Organization (NS-Frauenschaft) agreed to raise the money and recruit five thousand subscribers, it appeared that all obstacles had been overcome and Goebbels could begin work on the new format in November 1929. One problem, however, still remained.[35]

When Goebbels met with Amann and the Eher Verlag's printer, Adolf Mueller, on 21 November 1929, Amann's position had changed. He insisted that the new Berlin daily be a special edition of the *Voelkischer Beobachter*. Goebbels was appalled; he assigned this change of heart to Amann's unadulterated greed coupled with jealousy on the part of the editor of *Voelkischer Beobachter*, Alfred Rosenberg. The chief of Eher Verlag saw that a daily, if properly produced, could make a tremendous amount of money in a city of four million people. To make matters worse, Mueller would provide the printing presses for the new edition of the *Voelkischer Beobachter*, which would leave the publishers of *Der Angriff* without financial benefit from the new paper. Goebbels insisted that a paper with a style aimed primarily at the people of southern Germany would have little success in "Red Berlin." In the end, since the plan had Hitler's support, the party leadership adopted Amann's proposal. Publication of the Berlin edition of the *Voelkischer Beobachter* began on 1 March 1930. The paper, which was nothing more than the Munich edition with a one-page supplement containing Berlin news, was, as Goebbels anticipated, a failure, and Amann stopped publication little more than a year later.[36]

In spite of this serious defeat, the Berlin Nazi leader remained determined to publish his own daily and improve the Gau's propaganda apparatus. Goebbels continued to raise money for this project. Events began to turn in Goebbels's favor at the end of January 1930, when the Strassers' Kampfverlag began publication of a daily in Berlin without the approval of central party authorities. Issuance of a newspaper in direct competition to the official party organ was a serious action, which eventually contributed to the expulsion of Otto Strasser from the party, as well as the dissolution of the Kampfverlag. In the meantime, since the Strassers had a tremendous influence throughout northern Germany, Hitler was in desperate need of allies in Berlin.[37]

During this period of intra-party turmoil, Goebbels became increasingly disillusioned as Hitler hesitated to expel the Strassers from the party. Although the Gau leader would not allow the possibility of getting his own daily to fade, he did not actively pursue it during these difficult times; for this Hitler would be grateful. Goebbels's loyalty, coupled with the "electoral breakthrough" of September 1930, eventually bore fruit. On 26 September, the Berlin Gauleiter met with Amann to reach an agreement that would permit *Der Angriff* to begin publication six days per week.[38]

The two men formed a corporation, 60 percent owned by

Eher Verlag and the remainder by Angriff Verlag. The new daily would appear each afternoon at four beginning on 1 November and consist of ten pages. Both Amann and Goebbels benefited from the deal. The chief of Eher Verlag, since he owned the majority of the stock in the new corporation, would have financial control of the paper. Goebbels, on the other hand, received ideological command of the daily and would determine what was printed in the newspaper. He had created another valuable propaganda weapon. In addition, now that Kampfverlag was defunct, *Der Angriff* gained new prestige by becoming the official organ of Gau Berlin. After a protracted struggle, during which he had to overcome difficulties presented by both the central party leaders and the renegade Strassers, he had obtained his daily paper. *Der Angriff* would begin publication six days per week on 1 November 1930.[39]

The new daily newspaper, dubbed by Goebbels "The German Evening Newspaper in Berlin," presented its publisher with new opportunities. Now the Berlin NSDAP would have a chance to bring its ideas into the homes of party members Monday through Saturday. Some columns began to appear more regularly in the paper, for example a daily extract from a novel. The first serial that the daily published was Goebbels's novel, *Michael, Ein Deutsches Schicksal in Tagebuchblaettern*. Written in 1921, shortly after Goebbels received his doctorate from the University of Heidelberg and first published by the Eher Verlag in 1929, *Michael* is the story of a young university student who achieves *voelkisch* consciousness and, upon becoming dismayed about Germany's place in the post-Versailles world, commits suicide. In addition to the daily serial, the new format also included a sports section on page eight. Goebbels reduced the price of the paper to ten pfennigs. Later, *Der Angriff* expanded, once again, to twelve pages.[40]

The penchant to expand the size of newspaper, as well as include new columns during the years 1927-1933, is indicative of Goebbels's attitude toward both the role of the newspaper in Nazi propaganda and propaganda in general. The evolution of the pages of *Der Angriff* evince an increasing determination to present a Nazi view on everything. *Der Angriff* tried to nazify people's views not only on traditionally political matters—foreign policy, economics and domestic issues—but also within areas not traditionally thought of as being in the realm of politics: the role of women and the raising of children, books, music, and even sports. The Nazi world view had positions on all of these matters, and a newspaper was an effective means of propagating them. In short, *Der Angriff* was part of an attempt by the NSDAP to lay the foundation of a future totalitarian society; one in which the Fuehrer and his minions would have the last say on all matters, public and private, and no one would have the information necessary to oppose them. *Der Angriff*, and papers like it, would provide a valuable training ground for the future leaders of the Third Reich's propaganda apparatus, and this trend toward the creation of an all-encompassing world view would continue, indeed accelerate, during Hitler's years in power.

Although much information is available concerning *Der Angriff* as a propaganda tool, the same is not the case with the administrative history of the newspaper. There are no extant minutes of meetings of the organ's staff, and the only records available concerning discussions among the editors of the paper are Goebbels's brief diary entries. In spite of this lack of sources, there are some things which can be inferred about the way that the Gau leader ran his paper.

It is clear that until 1930 Goebbels was intimately involved in the operation of the newspaper. He wrote much of the copy himself, including the lead story and the "political diary," often preparing the former well in advance of publication in order to permit himself lengthy vacations. The publisher also played an active role in editing copy and laying out *Der Angriff*. Over time, he reduced his commitments in these areas, leaving them to those more temperamentally suited to regular work.[41]

Goebbels also attended conferences of the editorial staff. Whether the editors ever assembled without their boss is uncertain, but probable, since the publisher sometimes went several weeks without meeting with the staff. He did, however, usually meet with the editors two or three times per week to discuss management of the paper, taking particular care to emphasize ideological matters. The meager evidence available suggests that these gatherings were often unpleasant for everyone, especially Lippert, who was the focus of Goebbels's wrath. After informing the staff that he could only sacrifice seven or eight minutes of his time, Goebbels held the meetings in Lippert's office. Goebbels sat in the editor-in-chief's chair, forcing Lippert to stand as Goebbels berated him for incompetence, philosemitism, or being "bourgeois." Lippert was not the only victim of Goebbels's harangues, and no one, not even his good friend Schweitzer, was immune to his outbursts. After one of these eruptions, the business at hand completed, the Gauleiter would get up from his chair and walk out of the office.[42]

The permanent staff of *Der Angriff* did most of the day-to-day work of writing, editing, and laying out the newspaper. The editors of the various columns were the backbone of the staff, even writing most of the copy. At the outset, an almost complete lack of skilled journalists marred the quality of the paper. Eventually, as the employees gained valuable experience, the quality of the copy and the layout of the paper improved. As the paper expanded, appearing more often and adding new sections, the number of personnel employed by the newspaper increased. This was particularly true after *Der Angriff* became a daily in 1930.[43]

The financial condition of the newspaper was an almost constant concern to Goebbels and the staff, even after the party presented him with the funds to repay his original 2,000 RM loan. The number of readers remained low, and although Goebbels insisted that all party members subscribe, circulation was only about 4,500 in October 1927. In spite of the poor reception the paper received, Goebbels had to maintain the paper for two reasons. First, continuing publication of *Der Angriff* was a matter of prestige. The Gauleiter simply could not permit this newspaper to fail. Second, and perhaps more important, it was the only means he had, at least until the lifting of the ban on his speaking in public at the end of October 1927, of communicating with the membership. Although Goebbels required all party members to subscribe to *Der Angriff*, most did not. This eliminated what would have been a major source of funds. While the newspaper was a financial burden, it was yet another weapon against the hated system.[44]

Even as *Der Angriff* expanded and gained new readers, it remained insolvent. Goebbels's diaries record an almost unceasing series of financial crises at the office of the newspaper. After the ban against the Berlin NSDAP was lifted in 1928, the paper's solvency became intimately connected with that of the Gau organization. When the Gau was short of funds, *Der Angriff* suffered. Whenever it appeared that the Gau would have to declare bankruptcy or cease publication of the newspaper, a generous benefactor would provide the money necessary to avoid catastrophe. For example, in October 1928, the Gau received a gift of 25,000 RM from a person identified only as a "young man" named Haller. Another contributor gave Goebbels 10,000 RM in December 1929. It is clear, however, that Gau Berlin obtained most of the money necessary to operate the party organization and newspaper from the party rank and file.[45]

This constant struggle to maintain solvency helps to explain why Goebbels was willing to surrender some of his control of the newspaper to Amann when *Der Angriff* became a daily in 1930. Eher Verlag was committing its financial resources to the paper and as majority shareholder in *Der Angriff*, it had a financial responsibility to the Berlin organ. A promised salary of 12,000 RM for running the newspaper served as further incentive for Goebbels to make a deal.[46]

These measures, to the chagrin of the Berlin Nazi leader, did not ensure solvency. Even after the daily reached a circulation of eighty thousand in March 1931, making it the second largest Nazi organ after the *Voelkischer Beobachter*, financial problems plagued *Der Angriff*. By May 1931, the Gau was 18,000 RM in the red and Goebbels had been refused a loan of 20,000 RM for his newspaper. Even though *Der Angriff* showed a profit of 60,000 RM for 1932, the surplus went to retire the debts of the Gau and the newspaper. Throughout the Weimar period, the staff of *Der Angriff* found itself consistently on the verge of bankruptcy, and Goebbels never devised a means of assuring the solvency of his newspaper.[47]

Determining who read *Der Angriff* is difficult, because the staff never assembled the statistics necessary to do so. The paper never had a "letters to the editor" section. Therefore, it is not possible to canvas letters written to the organ in order to come to some conclusions, no matter how tenuous, concerning readership. Some hypotheses can be offered, however, based upon trends revealed in the Nazi press as a whole complemented by membership, election, and distribution statistics.

Historian Larry Wilcox has established a correlation between party membership and newspaper readership. The vast majority of readers of the Nazi press were committed National Socialists. In general, the press was not a means by which people were converted to the Nazi world view. As is usually the case today, people bought publications which related viewpoints they already possessed. A person first became a member of the NSDAP and then subscribed to the local party organ. This is established by the fact that, in general, large increases in the number of subscribers to the Nazi press followed rises in party membership. The number of subscribers never matched the massive electoral support the Nazis received after September 1930. Mere support for the Nazi program was not the determining factor in readership numbers; party membership was.[48]

The meager evidence available implies that the readership of *Der Angriff* fit these overall trends. Unfortunately, because a fire in 1934 destroyed many of *Der Angriff's* records, little information is available concerning circulation of the paper before 1930. There is some evidence, however, from which some overall trends can be inferred. Distribution remained low before September 1930, and the number of new subscribers recorded in Goebbels's diaries was quite small. In November 1928, for example, the Gauleiter was pleased with an increase of two hundred subscribers. In January 1929, he recorded an increase of three hundred. Whether this included the rise from November is not clear. Goebbels was pleased with these seemingly minor increases in circulation. This indicates that until 1930 *Der Angriff* had a small circulation and played a minor role in the political life of Berlin.[49]

As was the case in so many other areas of concern to the Nazi Party, the Reichstag election of 14 September 1930 was a turning point for the fortunes of *Der Angriff*. Nazi support in the capital city increased tenfold from the previous Reichstag election. In the May 1928 election, the Nazis received a mere 39,000 votes (1.6 percent of the votes cast); in September 1930, they received 396,000 (14.6 percent). Within the Reich as a whole, the NSDAP witnessed an increase of 2.6 to 18.3 percent. Hitler's party had become a major political force in the Weimar Republic.[50]

The "electoral breakthrough" brought an increase in party membership and with it a rise in the readership of the National Socialist press. *Der Angriff* was no exception to this trend. The paper became a daily in order to appeal to these new voters and party members. Circulation increased dramatically and approached 60,000 by the end of 1930, and in March 1931 it reached 80,000. Just before the 31 July 1932 Reichstag election when the Nazis received their best results (28.6 percent in Berlin and 37.4 percent in the Reich as a whole), the number of readers of *Der Angriff* reached its maximum at 110,600. Following the July 1932 elections, circulation of the Berlin paper began to decrease, anticipating the setback the Nazis would experience in the November 1932 elections. This provides further evidence that newspaper readership reflected party membership. After the July elections fewer people joined the NSDAP, and newspaper sales reflected this fact.[51]

The literature concerning the class membership of supporters of the NSDAP is voluminous, but determining the class to which the majority of readers of *Der Angriff* belonged with any certainty is a difficult task. The extant evidence is totally circumstantial. While it is clear that the editors of *Der Angriff* aimed their propaganda primarily at the working classes, it is impossible to prove that the readership of the paper was largely proletarian. Jeremy Brown has proved that the Berlin

NSDAP concentrated its activities in working-class districts of the city. Establishing that *Der Angriff* was aimed at the proletariat does not prove that most of its readers were workers. Additional circumstantial evidence, however, does make the contention that many workers read the paper appear more tenable. Historian Michael Kater has established that the Nazis made little headway within the urban proletariat before 1930. After the September 1930 elections an increasing number of workers joined the party. It was natural that a paper which had an editorial policy primarily aimed at the urban working class had an almost insignificant circulation before 1930. Few members of the middle classes would read a paper so clearly published to appeal to proletarians. Therefore, at least some of the immense increase in circulation of the paper can be assigned to a rise in the number of working-class readers. It is equally clear that an accompanying increase in the number of members from other social classes contributed to increases in circulation, and it would be irresponsible to assign the entire rise in readership after 1930 to newly-won proletarian readers.[52]

Whatever its source, the circulation of *Der Angriff* after 1930 made it a significant actor in Berlin politics. Each day Goebbels and his cohorts presented their agenda to as many as 110,000 readers from all walks of life. The editorial staff of the paper would try to make the most of this opportunity. *Der Angriff* was conceived in difficult times for the Berlin NSDAP. During the period 1927-1930, conditions improved only marginally. Even after the electoral breakthrough of September 1930, the newspaper remained a serious financial burden upon the party. On several occasions, *Der Angriff* was on the verge of bankruptcy, only to be saved by a generous donation. The editorial staff, however, could point to some successes. *Der Angriff* had helped to keep the party together during the difficult months of the prohibition. In addition, the paper had grown from its relatively modest origins to become the second largest Nazi-operated newspaper. This was quite an accomplishment.

3

The Party, the Fuehrer Myth, and the Presidential Election

From the publication of its first issue in July 1927, *Der Angriff* played an important role in Nazi intra-party politics. Goebbels had founded his newspaper, in part, to enable him to undermine the Strassers' *Berliner Arbeiter Zeitung*. The Gauleiter simply could not tolerate its existence; a paper beyond his control was an affront to his position as leader of Berlin's Nazis. Since Hitler had decreed that the National Socialist press could not publish personal attacks upon party members, Goebbels's assault upon the BAZ and its publishers could not be made on the pages of *Der Angriff*. He had to find other means.[1]

Goebbels started a newspaper war. He began by refusing to give the BAZ information concerning Gau meetings. Hence, any Nazi seeking a schedule of Berlin party functions would have to turn to the district leader's own organ. In addition, Goebbels used the SA to intimidate sellers of the BAZ. Storm troopers in civilian clothes assaulted Strasser supporters, causing several of them to move out of the city. In spite of the Kampfverlag's protestations to the Fuehrer, Hitler refused to discipline Goebbels, making it obvious that the Berlin Gauleiter was acting in accord with Hitler's wishes. Clearly, the Fuehrer was determined to destroy the Nazi "left" at the first available opportunity.[2]

Goebbels's campaign against the BAZ worked; circulation of the Kampfverlag organ decreased dramatically throughout northern Germany. Not only did *Der Angriff* offer the only source of information about party functions, but it had a more dynamic style. The BAZ attempted to appeal to the capital's working-classes in a "rational," somewhat intellectual, manner. *Der Angriff* took a different, more emotional, approach. Nazi readers found Schweitzer's depiction of the ideal National Socialist—a muscular worker with an unbuttoned shirt and a hammer in his hand—more compelling than the somewhat dry reading found in the BAZ. Goebbels's newspaper soon became the *de facto* organ of the Gau Gross-Berlin. The BAZ, although it was the official district newspaper, simply could not compete with the Gau leader's organization.[3]

The summer of 1928 saw further developments that would have a dramatic impact upon the Goebbels-Strasser feud. The Nazis did poorly in national elections, which discredited the "urban plan," under which the NSDAP had tried to appeal to Germany's proletariat, in the eyes of many leading Nazis. With the development of a new electoral strategy, which would attempt to appeal to the peasantry, the Nazi left lost much of its influence in the movement. The Kampfverlag, however, refused to accept its decline peacefully. While the rest of the leadership contended that attempts to appeal to the proletariat had failed and might not prove fruitful in the future, Otto Strasser argued that the party's refusal to adopt truly socialist principles had caused the electoral failure of 1928. He called for the establishment of a National Socialist trade union, a move that was anathema to orthodox Nazis. Gregor Strasser, on the other hand, realized that new campaign strategies had to be adopted, and the years 1928-1930 saw him drift gradually to the right. He began to distance himself from his erstwhile colleagues on the left and, in 1928, accepted the powerful post of organization leader, overseeing the party bureaucracy.[4]

With the influence of the Strasser group reaching its nadir, Hitler found himself in a position where he could increase pressure upon the Kampfverlag. He did nothing, for example, when Goebbels declared *Der Angriff* the Berlin NSDAP's "district organ." In addition, when Otto Strasser refused to surrender in the face of almost constant harassment by the Berlin SA, the Fuehrer traveled to Berlin to meet with his intransigent subordinate. Surprising the younger Strasser by bursting into his flat unannounced, Hitler demanded that the Kampfverlag submit to Goebbels's authority. Strasser told Hitler that he would not back down in the face of threats from the Gauleiter's hooligans. Further, he threatened that he had a revolver in his desk drawer and would not hesitate to use it on his visitor. Hitler, realizing that there was nothing that he could do to cow Strasser, stormed out of the room. The Fuehrer, however, did not give up. In 1929, while Otto Strasser was in Munich, Hitler offered to purchase Kampfverlag, but Strasser refused to sell it.[5]

Two things occurred in the spring and summer of 1930 that forced Hitler's hand. First, in March 1930, Kampfverlag began publishing a daily in Berlin, *Der Nationalsozialist*, in defiance of Hitler's wishes. Amann, speaking for Hitler, agreed with Goebbels that Otto Strasser's new paper, a competitor for both *Der Angriff* and the Berlin edition of the *Voelkischer Beobachter*, must be eliminated. The Berlin Gau leader and the chief of Eher Verlag got their chance to do so because of a tactical mistake on Otto Strasser's part in April. The *Saechsischer Beobachter*, a Kampfverlag paper, supported a strike by Saxon metalworkers, violating the party's officially neutral position on the issue. Hitler had had enough, and he gave Goebbels *carte blanche* in his assault on Strasser and his newspaper apparatus.[6]

Hitler ordered Goebbels to begin *"ruthlessly* [to] *clean up* the party of all those [Strasserite] elements in Berlin," an assignment the Berlin Nazi leader accepted happily. While the Berlin SA intensified its harassment of Nazi leftists, the Fuehrer did his part to assist the storm troopers. In May, he told the national party court to dismiss a case Strasser had brought against the business manager of Gau Berlin in response to assaults upon sellers of the BAZ. On 30 and 31 May Hitler met with Otto Strasser in the Hotel Sanssouci, where the Fuehrer was staying. According to Strasser's account of the discussions, Hitler harangued him for several hours, insisting that Strasser submit to his authority and sell the

Kampfverlag to the party. Otto Strasser, who had become *de facto* chief of Kampfverlag since Gregor's defection, refused to meet either demand. As a result Berlin's assault upon the ideological heresy intensified, and Goebbels began purging Strasser's supporters.[7]

On 30 June 1930 Gregor Strasser announced his resignation from all his positions with the Kampfverlag, and the NSDAP officially severed all ties with the press organization. In order to keep his position as organization leader, Gregor Strasser agreed never to have further contact, either personally or politically, with his brother. Further, Hitler sent a letter to Goebbels granting his district leader the right to hold an all-Gau meeting at which Goebbels could deal with the dissidents. The assembly took place on 2 July. Otto Strasser was invited, but the SA guard at the door refused to admit him. Goebbels expelled several Strasser supporters at the assembly, causing Otto to issue an ultimatum to the Fuehrer. He demanded that Hitler rescind the Gauleiter's expulsions and, when he received no answer from the Nazi leader, resigned from the NSDAP on 4 July 1930, selling Kampfverlag to the party. Otto Strasser and his supporters exited the party under the slogan "The Socialists have left the NSDAP," delivering a serious blow to radicalism within the party.[8]

Otto Strasser founded his own political party, the Kampfgemeinschaft revolutionaerer Nationalsozialisten (Struggling Community of Revolutionary National Socialists), also known as the "Black Front." The goal of the movement was to establish a type of *voelkisch* socialism through the creation of nationalist trade unions and other working-class organizations. In short, the Kampfgemeinschaft, completely ignoring the peasantry, pursued the same policies as the NSDAP had before the electoral debacle of 1928. They would prove even less effective than earlier Nazi attempts to attract the proletariat. Otto Strasser led 5,000 people out of the NSDAP in July 1930, none of whom was an important Nazi leader. In September 1930, Strasser could claim only 260 supporters in the German capital, once a center of the Nazi left. Although the number of members would not peak until April 1931, the Kampfgemeinschaft never posed a serious threat to the NSDAP. Also, the official organ of Strasser's group, *Der Nationalsozialist*, having only four thousand readers, was never a serious competitor for *Der Angriff.*[9]

Now that Otto Strasser had left the party, Goebbels could openly attack him. *Rote Fahne* reported that the Gauleiter had ordered the SA to "beat them [the Strasserites] down!" Although violence against members of the organization was rampant, the Communist daily had no sympathy for the ex-Nazis.[10]

Goebbels could now begin an offensive against Strasser in his newspaper as well, publishing a story entitled "The Eternal Critic" in the 6 July 1930 edition of *Der Angriff*. Although the Gauleiter did not mention Otto Strasser and his supporters by name, it is clear that they were the subject of the article. These "Jammergestalten" ("pitiable figures") had refused to work for the benefit of Germany and wished to turn the NSDAP into a debating society. Their primary goal was the criticism of Hitler and the other leaders of the movement, not the creation of a National Socialist Germany. In response, the party should look to the "old guard" for direction. These men had been members of the Nazi Party since its creation, and only they knew what the party stood for—action. This did not imply, Goebbels continued, that the leadership did not have an "open ear" for suggestions from the membership. Indeed, the party benefited from honest criticism aimed at improving its fortunes. Attacks, however, aimed at the destruction of National Socialism could not be tolerated. Those "eternal critics" who wished to usurp the legitimate powers of the old guard had to be expelled; the party leadership had done the NSDAP a valuable service by doing so.[11]

The "Political Diary" of the same issue contained another essay, also written by Goebbels, concerning the Strasser controversy. Here, the paper's publisher insisted that Strasser and his minions had striven to discredit the "25 Point Program" of the party in order to implement their own. This destructive agenda had to be derailed. The party had done that. Once again, Goebbels insisted that, to these men, "dis-

cussion was an end in itself," and all men of action must re-
ject this notion. The party had to impose discipline and had
rightfully done so.[12]

These two articles shared common themes that the Berlin
Gau leader hoped would convince his readers that the break
had been Otto Strasser's fault. The Strasser camp, not the
Hitlerites, as the dissidents claimed, had betrayed the ideals of
National Socialism. They had denounced the party program
and violated the trust of the Fuehrer. The people who had remained in the party, whose ideological roots went back to the
creation of the NSDAP, were the true National Socialists. Goebbels also stressed a prominent theme of Nazi propaganda: the
Nazis were the party of action. Hitler and his supporters did
something. They assaulted the system. Otto Strasser had
bought into that Bolshevik-dominated system with his call for
more socialism. In short, the supporters of Hitler represented
the true goals of National Socialism, not the Black Front.

The tenor of the Gau Leader's attacks says something
about the real roots of the dispute. In the end, Hitler did not
run Otto Strasser and the Nazi left out of the party as the
result of a debate over a new propaganda strategy. While the
period after the 1928 election did see the Nazis increase their
appeals to the peasantry, they never did give up on the proletariat.[13] What the Fuehrer found objectionable in the actions
of the Strasser camp, and Goebbels echoed this, was its refusal to submit to the party leadership, to accept the infallibility
of Hitler's decisions. The debate over propaganda strategy
was simply a pretext for a final reckoning with the left. In
short, Otto Strasser had been tricked into starting a fight
that he could not win.

Goebbels's newspaper had emerged from the Hitler-Strasser dispute with an improved position in party circles. The
Kampfverlag was defunct. The *BAZ* was no longer a serious
competitor for *Der Angriff* because it could not claim to repre-
sent the positions of the party's national leadership. *Der Angriff* had remained true to the goals of the party and was not
tainted by ideological heresy as was the *BAZ*. In addition,
Goebbels's paper became the new official organ of Gau Berlin,

thereby gaining new prestige. Because its publisher had fought on the front lines of this party dispute, Hitler decided to permit Goebbels to begin daily publication in November 1930.[14]

Even more important than the paper's role in intra-party feuds was its part in communicating with party members and potential Nazis. In order to win and maintain supporters, *Der Angriff* had to define exactly what National Socialism was and what it stood for. The most interesting perspective from which to examine this issue is an analysis of the role of the newspaper during the period of the prohibition of the Berlin NSDAP, May 1927 to April 1928. During this eleven-month span, party meetings were forbidden and Gau Berlin was in serious danger of dissolution, and *Der Angriff* was the only means by which Goebbels could communicate with the membership. Therefore, the way in which the paper presented the party to its readers was of the utmost importance.

Among the most important things the staff of *Der Angriff* did during the prohibition was to assure party members that the NSDAP was still active in the capital. If the rank and file believed that Nazism was dead in Berlin, the party would lose members and eventually dissolve. Hence, *Der Angriff* tried to maintain the morale of the now illegal party by assuring its readers that National Socialism would not surrender, as the hated Weimar system wanted. In one of Goebbels's front-page articles, published in August 1927, the Gau leader promised his readers that "We will not surrender!" He went on to assure them that the NSDAP had pledged itself to "love an enslaved people" and fight for its freedom. "So we are [still] committed," he wrote. Although a "strike of the pen marked us out of existence," the Berlin Nazis would never capitulate. They would continue to fight for the liberation of the Fatherland. "*Schlag zu! Schlag zu!* [Attack! Attack!]" he continued. "We will not surrender!"[15]

In keeping with this theme, *Der Angriff* made a concerted effort to show that, in spite of the prohibition, the NSDAP was still strong. The August 1927 party congress in Nuremberg presented an excellent chance to make this case. The paper emphasized the large crowds, estimated at 100,000, present for the party rally. It contended that Berlin's Nazi Party was strongly represented, in spite of its underground status. Seats on the "special train" to Nuremberg were "sold out," evincing that the ban could not "exterminate the spirit" of the movement. Since the article did not give an estimate of the number of those attending, it is probable that it was relatively small. *Der Angriff* had made it clear, however, that the Berlin NSDAP was not defunct.[16]

The staff of *Der Angriff* made an effort to use the hardships that the prohibition had imposed upon party members as a propaganda tool. The paper's copy recorded the "persecution" and the "sentences under Jewish law" to which the system had subjugated Berlin's Nazis. As was the case with early Christianity, this persecution would only serve to strengthen the movement and increase its size. In the end, they warned, the Weimar authorities would lose.[17]

This was a popular theme in the caricatures of cartoonist Hans Schweitzer. For example, an August 1927 cartoon showed a chained arm holding a Nazi flag. In the background was the Brandenburg Gate. The caption said, in large letters, "BERLIN! TROTZ VERBOT—NICHT TOT! [Not dead—despite prohibition!]" A March 1928 cartoon showed the vice president of the Berlin Police, Bernhard Weiss, throwing seeds into a field. Above the seeds was written the words "Persecution," "Prohibitions," "Prison Terms," and "Maltreatment." Growing in the field, the result of the misdeeds sown by Weiss, were SA men. The caption read, "Whoever sows the wind, will reap a whirlwind—!" The prohibition would, in the long run, only strengthen the party.[18]

Der Angriff also tried to make it clear that the Berlin party leadership was fighting the prohibition which had brought such hardship upon the rank and file. In August 1927, perhaps in part to boost its lagging sales, an article in *Der Angriff* reminded readers that the paper had been founded specifically to fight the *Verbot*. It was "the best weapon" against the system that the movement had. "They [Berlin's authorities] have forbidden us the spoken word. Now we fight with the pen and printing press." The message was clear: all Nazis who wished to maintain contact with the now illegal movement should become subscribers to *Der Angriff*. The paper also recorded how Goebbels had taken the Berlin Police force to court in order to have the ban lifted. The court decided that since, in its view, the Berlin party organization was totally independent of any national political party, the prohibition was legal. *Der Angriff* assured its readers that National Socialism would not be subject to "Jewish law" and the fight would continue. The party would never give up.[19]

The persistence of the Berlin Nazi Party paid off. On 31 March 1928, faced with the fact that he could not effectively enforce the prohibition, the president of the Berlin Police, Karl Zoergiebel, lifted the ban. On 13 April, Goebbels officially reestablished Gau Berlin in an "overfilled hall." In the "Political Diary" of the following week, he recorded that "It is almost like a dream!" An "electric" atmosphere permeated the room. The doors "sprung open," and a company of "soldiers in brown marched" down the aisle "in unison." The Nazi flag was legally exhibited for the first time in almost a year. It had returned as all true believers knew it would. Goebbels concluded the piece with a jubilant verse:

> As we march
> God stands at our side.
> He wants, and so should it be,
> That right will be victorious.[20]

Now that the prohibition had ended, the party had to surrender one of its most effective propaganda themes and would have to devise others.

During the summer of 1928 the Berlin organ turned to a new propaganda campaign. During July, *Der Angriff* published three articles, all written by Goebbels, outlining the basic tenets of National Socialism. Goebbels undoubtedly hoped that these pieces could help win converts to the movement.

The first of these articles, an obvious attempt to appeal to members of other *voelkisch* groups, related the Nazi definition of nationalism. Being a "nationalist," Goebbels contended, had nothing to do with being loyal to a "form of government" or "symbol of the state." It was a matter of dedication to the *Volk*. It was racist. The problem with "bourgeois patriotism" was that it did not recognize this fact. On the other hand, supporters of the "reactionary right" had in mind not the interests of the *Volk* but those of a former ruling class, those of the Kaiser. Hence, this was not, the article continued, nationalism at all. By implication, Goebbels was stating that the Nazis were the only true nationalists in Germany because they, of all political factions, had the interests of the nation, the *Volk*, at heart.[21]

The following week Goebbels attempted to present a Nazi definition of socialism. Socialism was, he argued, the belief that society should pursue the advantage of all. He considered only *Volksgenossen* (racial comrades) to be legitimate members of German society. Therefore, Jews could never be true socialists. They were advocates of Marxism only because it aggravated the class divisions within the *Volk* that kept the Jews in power. In an obvious attempt to court proletarian support, Goebbels continued by stating that capitalism was equally bankrupt because it supported the bourgeoisie at the expense of the working class. This also contributed to unhealthy class divisions. True socialism was a middle way between capitalism and Marxism that would place the interests of Germany above class antagonisms. The NSDAP, a strong advocate of putting an end to class conflict, was the only truly socialist party.[22]

Two weeks later the Gau leader published an article dealing with what was the most important tenet of National Socialism, anti-Semitism. In this article, a clear attempt to appeal to the traditional right, Goebbels made sweeping generalizations, blaming the Jews for all Germany's ills. Of course, he made no effort to present evidence justifying his absurd claims. Nazis hated the Jew because he had "injured the social necessities of the general population" through the promotion of cleavages in German society. He had also contaminated the German race. Because of this, "we can thank him for the fact that we are today the pariahs of the entire world." In addition, the Jew was "not creative." He did not work but lived off the labor of others. Goebbels concluded by linking national-ism and socialism with hatred of Jews. True socialism would cast the Jews out of Germany in order to eliminate all class hatred, which was the product of an insidious Jewish con-spiracy. A true nationalist concerns himself with the racial purity of the German *Volk* and opposes Jewish efforts to pol-lute Germany's blood. For these two reasons, Goebbels ar-gued, any National Socialist must be an anti-Semite. He concluded by dismissing humane concerns for Germany's Jewish population. The crimes of the Jews made them less than human and not subject to Christian charity. They de-served only persecution, and the NSDAP was willing to pro-vide it.[23]

To the average German, however, the party's ideology was not its most important asset; its Fuehrer was. Hitler possessed a charismatic personality unequaled by the leader of any other political faction. His personality would make the National Socialist Party a viable force in German politics. During the time of struggle, Nazi propaganda began creating a "Fuehrer myth" surrounding the personality of Hitler, claiming that he was the solution to all of Germany's problems.[24]

Der Angriff made a valuable contribution to the creation of the Hitler myth. Drawings of the Fuehrer, and sometimes ex-pensive photographs, were a regular feature of the paper. For example, the 23 April 1928 issue contained a drawing of Hitler, a determined look on his face, with the upraised arms of his followers in the background. The caption read, "Freedom is not yet lost." Hitler always appeared with a serious counte-nance, the problems of Germany his constant concern.[25]

The 1927 party rally presented the editors of *Der Angriff* with an opportunity to enhance the image of the Fuehrer. In the issue dealing with the rally, the paper published a piece written by Houston Stewart Chamberlain entitled "The Pic-ture of the Leader." Hitler, Chamberlain wrote, was a man of integrity who "looked his audience in the eye" when he made a promise. He was not a liar. He was also a great leader who would save Germany from its despair because he knew about economics, foreign policy, and the "problems of the people."

Der Führer spricht!

"The Fuehrer speaks!" (All illustrations are from *Der Angriff*.)

In short, he was the solution to all of Germany's problems. The next issue published a drawing of Hitler speaking to the 100,000 Nazis present at the rally. As Hitler spoke, assuming a dramatic pose, the audience was enthralled. He was a leader of the masses who could communicate with them.[26]

A visit to Berlin by the Fuehrer was a major propaganda event. One such occasion, recorded in dramatic fashion on the pages of *Der Angriff*, was in July 1928. The evening began with a parade of the SA through Friedrichshain, passers-by soon joining the storm troopers. When they arrived at the hall at 7:30 P.M., the paper's account continued, it was already full. At 8:00 P.M. a film about the 1927 Nuremberg rally was shown. As it concluded, there was "suddenly an outcry of the thousands of spectators: Hitler—Hitler!" After a brief introduction by Goebbels, the evening's events came to a climax with the Fuehrer's speech. It was a typical Hitler performance, beginning with a critique of Weimar Germany's foreign policy, which had brought Germany so much disgrace. He then turned to an attack upon bourgeois elements who acquiesced in the emasculation of Germany. In response to threats from other European powers, Hitler proposed an alliance with Fascist Italy. The speech concluded with a call to stand behind the party in its struggle to return Germany to its rightful place in European affairs. The evening ended with yet another parade through the streets of the German capital. The article concluded with the statement: "A great day in the history of the movement in Berlin was over."[27]

Although the Hitler visit had ended, the beneficial propaganda it brought had not. The 6 August edition of *Der Angriff* published a story recording that Hitler's Berlin speech had been covered in the Italian press. The paper, *Journal of Italy*, gave the speech a positive review, recording that throughout the three-hour speech, "one did not hear anyone breathe." Although Hitler's call for a German-Italian alliance was not mentioned, the Italians did applaud his insistence upon an end to all diplomatic ties with Bolshevik Russia. The purpose of this article was clear. *Der Angriff* wished to convey the fact that the movement received attention outside of Germany, that it was becoming an important actor in European political affairs. This was the case because of the Fuehrer.[28]

The Berlin organ also made a concerted effort to counter frequent attacks made upon Hitler's character. On 22 January 1928, for example, the newspaper *Reichsbanner* published a story about a man, Mr. Julian, who claimed that Hitler was a Jew. *Der Angriff* dismissed the charge out of hand. After all, Obersdorf, where *Reichsbanner* was published, was populated primarily by Poles, not members of the *Volk*. *Der Angriff* dismissed the paper as a "comical" propaganda organ of the SPD. In a manner typical of the Berlin Nazi paper, it attacked the character of the person making charges against Hitler, rather than presenting evidence to refute them.[29]

The 1932 presidential campaign provided *Der Angriff* with its greatest opportunity to build the Hitler myth. During the spring of that year, there were two presidential elections that pitted Hitler against the popular incumbent, Field Marshal Otto von Hindenburg, as well as the Communist leader, Ernst Thaelmann. The Nazi Fuehrer, because of his status as the leader of what was, by now, the second-largest party in Germany, received much attention. *Der Angriff* decided to seize this opportunity to enhance Hitler's image as well as attack opponents of National Socialism.

The election was the result of Chancellor Heinrich Bruening's failed attempt to have the aging president's term extended. It was to end in the spring of 1932. While it was generally agreed that Hindenburg would easily win reelection should a contest be held, Bruening and his supporters feared that the eighty-four-year-old field marshal would not survive the rigors of a campaign. The chancellor developed a plan under which a two-thirds vote of the Reichstag would override the constitution and extend Hindenburg's term. Since the KPD would certainly oppose the proposal, Bruening needed to secure the support of the right in order to get the measure through the Reichstag. Alfred Hugenberg, leader of the Nationalists, refused to support the bill outright. Hitler, on the other hand, made certain demands that Bruening would have to meet in order to secure Nazi support. Bruening had to lift all bans and prohibitions placed upon the NSDAP throughout the Reich as well as dissolve the Reichstag and call for new elections. In addition, Hindenburg would have to dismiss Bruening (Hitler hoped to secure the chancellorship for himself). The chancellor, of course, could not accept this last demand. Talks between Bruening and the NSDAP collapsed, and an election became imminent.[30]

At first it appeared that Hindenburg would not stand for reelection. There were several reasons for his hesitation. First, he feared that he was too old to endure the stress of a campaign. Bruening circumvented this problem by agreeing to do all of the president's campaigning for him. Hindenburg would make but one radio address. The incumbent also resented the fact that he would have to rely upon the support of the SPD—a party which, as a traditional conservative, he detested—in order to assure victory. He seriously considered forgoing running in order to avoid such a distasteful proposition. Bruening, however, pointed out that the only viable alternative to a Hindenburg presidency was a Hitler administration, which the field marshal found more distasteful than courting Socialist support. Finally, the chancellor devised a plan under which a Hindenburg reelection would be a prelude to a restoration of the monarchy, a possibility the reactionary Hindenburg simply could not ignore. Because of Bruening's convincing arguments, Hindenburg announced his candidacy on 16 February 1932.[31]

The incumbent was not the only popular politician who hesitated to run for the presidency. Hindenburg seemed unbeatable, and Hitler feared losing a major election, which could break the NSDAP's momentum. On the other hand, if the Fuehrer, leader of Germany's second-largest party, refused to stand, it would look as if he had backed away from a challenge, a conclusion he wanted to avoid at all costs. Hitler was in a quandary, and Goebbels was instrumental in helping him reach a decision.[32]

As early as the middle of January 1932, the Berlin Gau leader had begun to urge Hitler to announce his candidacy. In addition to contending that the Fuehrer could not bypass such an important contest, Goebbels honestly believed that Hitler could win. He went so far as to use *Der Angriff* to persuade his leader to make the desired decision. The 30 January 1932 edition of the paper had as its headline "Spontaneous Ovation in Sportpalast for Adolf Hitler." The accompanying story told of a crowd of ten thousand Nazis chanting "Hitler for president!" The loyal supporters of the NSDAP had made their feelings clear, and Hitler could not deny the will of the masses, agreeing to run on 2 February. Goebbels, however, decided upon a strategy aimed at maintaining a feeling of suspense about Hitler's decision; the question remained, would Hitler run? On 22 February Goebbels ended the tension by announcing the Fuehrer's candidacy before a packed house in Berlin's Sportpalast. Goebbels hoped that the approaching campaign, which he would oversee, would be "a masterpiece in the way of propaganda." Under his auspices, it would be extremely well organized. The staffs of the dozens of Nazi newspapers throughout Germany worked together in order to increase the effectiveness of the Nazi press apparatus. People all over the Reich read the same copy on the same day. Goebbels strived to make maximum use of his limited resources. The presidential campaign would be the most co-ordinated in the NSDAP's history.[33]

The Nazis, of course, were not the only party that campaigned during the two presidential contests. Hindenburg and the parties behind him also had an effective propaganda apparatus. The theme of the incumbent's campaign was one that concentrated upon Hindenburg's character and his ability to provide stability in troubled times. In contrast, if Hitler were elected president, his administration would bring "hate, partisanship, inexperience, government by party 'hacks,' self-destruction and further deterioration of the German people" and even civil war. Further, a vote for Ernst Thaelmann, candidate of the KPD, was the same as a vote for Hitler since the Communist candidate had no chance of winning. Hindenburg's propaganda largely ignored the other candidate, Theodor Duesterberg, representing the right-wing "Harzburg Front"; none of the three leading candidates considered him a threat.[34]

Ironically, Thaelmann's campaign had a similar theme to that of Hindenburg: "Whoever votes for Hindenburg, votes for Hitler, whoever votes for Hitler votes for war!" The Communists insisted that there was no substantial difference between Hitler and Hindenburg. They were both fascist representatives of the capitalist elite that was responsible for the plight of Germany's proletariat. The only real alternative to the miserable status quo was Thaelmann.[35]

On 20 February 1932, Goebbels distributed a letter that outlined Nazi campaign strategy for the 13 March election. It emphasized that party propaganda would concentrate upon attacking the status quo rather than present a positive program for ending Germany's problems. Goebbels took this path for a variety of reasons. First, Hindenburg was tremendously popular within all strata of the German population, especially among the right-wing groups to whom the Nazis hoped to appeal. Attacking him personally could be counterproductive. In addition, the economic situation was so desperate in Germany that the NSDAP was hoping to benefit from the dissatisfaction rampant within all classes. Finally, negative campaigning eliminated the necessity of presenting concrete solutions to Germany's problems, something Goebbels and other Nazi leaders wished to avoid.[36]

Der Angriff reflected Goebbels's attitudes toward the campaign, concentrating its attacks upon the Weimar system. These assaults can be put into two categories: attacks upon Hitler's opponents and charges against the Bruening government. The third pillar of Goebbels's election strategy was the promotion of Hitler's personality. This would, however, remain a secondary consideration in the 13 March campaign.

An important part of any political crusade, especially for the National Socialists, was to discredit one's opponents. Hindenburg, however, presented a special problem in this regard. He was the hero of Tannenberg, a symbol of their country's past to all Germans. That Hitler, a mere corporal in the war, should run against the great field marshal could cause the Nazis to lose support among *voelkisch* elements. Goebbels recognized this problem, recording in his diary that "the honorable personality of the president of the Reich is shamelessly being dragged into the fight. Now we must be clever!" Hitler also recognized this problem when he stated that "one should never deprive the volk of its gods." Goebbels sought to resolve this problem by attacking the supporters of Hindenburg rather than the president himself.[37]

This strategy can be seen in the pages of *Der Angriff* even before the campaign officially began. The 23 January issue contained an editorial written by Goebbels protesting Zoergiebel's recent banning of *Der Angriff*. The police president had done so under the auspices of a presidential decree signed, naturally, by Hindenburg. "Does he [Hindenburg] want to suffer having his name used in such a manner again?" No, the paper concluded, because his affinity for "truth and justice" would forbid it.[38]

The practice of not attacking the president directly, but rather concentrating the Nazi assault upon his supporters, continued into the presidential campaign. On 15 February, a front-page cartoon depicted Hindenburg riding on the back of Thaelmann, implying that he had KPD support. The cartoon was entitled "His 'Train to Victory.'" The 23 February number of *Der Angriff* featured Jewish caricatures holding Hindenburg posters, emphasizing the Nazi claim that the "Jewish world conspiracy" stood behind the forces supporting the president and the Weimar system. Indeed, because he had heeded the advice of his "Jewish" backers, Hindenburg bore responsibility for the 6 million Germans who lost their jobs because of the depression.[39]

Goebbels's newspaper also dubbed the field marshal "the candidate of the Social Democrats," a title that the staunchly conservative President undoubtedly found insulting. Throughout the campaign, *Der Angriff* emphasized the fact that the SPD, the party of the November Criminals and the system, stood behind the incumbent. A vote for Hindenburg was a vote for the status quo and all of the evils inherent in the system. *Der Angriff* pursued this policy, all the time emphasizing that "the personality of Reichspresident Hindenburg is unassailable for us also."[40]

Thaelmann, the candidate of the hated KPD, was the victim of even more vicious insults than Hindenburg. *Der Angriff* insisted that he was "not the leader of the German proletariat . . . He is the caretaker of the Russian leadership and can only do anything on its orders. . . . Thaelmann can never be a leader, because he is not allowed to have any of his own opinions."[41] He was, in short, an agent of a foreign power determined to bring revolution and class warfare to Germany.

Duesterberg, having no chance of winning, received the least amount of attention in *Der Angriff*. The paper portrayed him as the candidate of the *Reaktion*, a mere pawn of big business. He would not fight for the common man as would Hitler.[42]

Slightly over 37 million (3,425,750 in Berlin) Germans went to the polls on Sunday, 13 March 1932. Hindenburg, as almost everyone expected, received a plurality of the votes cast, 18,650,000 (1,307,661 in the capital). Hitler was second with 11,400,000 (666,053 in Berlin, placing him third in the city). The Communist candidate, Thaelmann, got 5,000,000 votes (685,411 in the capital city) and Duesterberg a mere 2,500,000 (232,224 in Berlin). The only surprise was that Hindenburg failed to get the requisite majority of the votes cast needed under the Weimar constitution to secure reelection. There would have to be a runoff election, which Chancellor Bruening scheduled for 10 April 1932.[43]

Goebbels, as always, strived to turn defeat into victory. *Der Angriff* dealt with the setback optimistically. The headline on 14 March read, "Majority of the People Against Hindenburg— NSDAP Support Doubles!" Since the incumbent was the candidate of the status quo, the fact that he had failed to receive a majority of the votes cast was a scathing indictment of the system. Repeating a popular campaign theme, *Der Angriff* maintained that, since the Communists had lost votes since the last Reichstag election, Marxists were voting for Hindenburg. The paper also emphasized the fact that the number of votes Hitler received was double the Nazi support in the September 1930 election. A story on 15 March reminded readers that all parties except the NSDAP had lost votes since 1930.[44]

Though it was clear that Hindenburg would have little trouble securing reelection—a plurality of the votes cast was all that was needed to win the runoff election—Goebbels had to get the Nazi propaganda machine ready for another campaign. He outlined his press strategy in a circular that appeared on 23 March 1932. After ordering that all Nazi papers distribute special election editions on 29 March, he turned to the theme of the second contest: the character of the Fuehrer. All Nazi organs were to have a "unified theme" on specified days beginning 29 March. On that day, the motif upon which the entire Nazi press apparatus was to concentrate was "Hitler as a man." The subject of the following day would be "Hitler as comrade." On 31 March the National Socialist press would concentrate its efforts upon depicting "Hitler as political fighter." The first day of April would see Nazi newspapers present "Hitler as statesman."[45] While appeals to the personality cult surrounding Hitler were not absent during the first campaign, Goebbels and *Der Angriff* would adopt them as their central theme during the second contest, doing much to contribute to the creation of the Hitler myth.

Emphasizing Hitler's personality, however, was not the

only Nazi strategy in the second campaign. *Der Angriff* also emphasized the inevitability of a Nazi victory. The number of Nazi supporters, it alleged, increased daily. There was, as a result of NSDAP election victories, "Desperation within the Communist 'Masses.'" Many erstwhile Communist voters, the paper alleged, who would refuse to support the doomed candidacy of Ernst Thaelmann, had been forced by economic circumstances to accept the "ideas of our Fuehrer and . . . become nationalists." Typical of this tactic was the publication of a letter from a former Communist explaining his conversion to Nazism: "There is no other way for me."[46]

The 31 March edition of *Der Angriff* carried reports of yet more conversions to National Socialism. Since Duesterberg had withdrawn his candidacy in light of his poor showing, the Stahlhelm, the Nationalist paramilitary group, had given its support to Hitler. This made the Nazi leader the "National Unity Candidate" of all those who rejected the system. If all right-wing groups, the paper insisted, fell in line behind Hitler as the Stahlhelm had, the Fuehrer would win the election, and Germany would be saved.[47]

The primary source of the popularity of National Socialism was, of course, Adolf Hitler. His magnetic personality was the movement's primary asset, and Goebbels made the most of it during the second contest. On 31 March, an article appeared in *Der Angriff* entitled "Hitler, the Political Fighter." Written by Goebbels, it was a brief biography of the Nazi leader. At the end of the First World War the Fuehrer had vowed to avenge the crimes of November 1918 and had struggled against the system created by the November Criminals ever since. Hitler had become "a symbol of Germany's rebirth for the wide masses." Eleven and one-half million Nazi voters in the March election was proof; there was simply no stopping Hitler's momentum.[48]

On 3 April Hitler began his famous aerial campaign tour of Germany. *Der Angriff* reported that, in the course of this campaign, entitled "Hitler over Germany," the Nazi leader would speak to 1 million Germans, visiting twenty-one cities in six days. A reporter for the paper, having been in the

Fuehrer's plane, wrote that, as Germany faded beneath them, they realized that Hitler and his entourage had embarked upon a historic mission, and German politics had never witnessed anything comparable.[49]

Hitler's "Flight over Germany" began a new emphasis in *Der Angriff's* approach to the campaign. In this second contest, the paper concentrated not only upon the speakers at Hitler rallies but also upon the crowds. It tried to transform the mass hysteria of a Nazi meeting into print. Therefore, the organ published articles such as "80,000 in Dresden," "60,000 in Potsdam," and "20,000 in the Sportpalast." These pieces contained reports of tens of thousands raising their arms in the Hitler salute upon seeing their hope for the future. Women cried. Hitler kissed babies.[50]

Der Angriff and other Nazi papers portrayed Hitler as a man of the people. The article, "Adolf Hitler, the man" presented him as a leader whose primary motivation was the love of his people. He was "not only a politician, but a common man . . . to whom millions have given their last hope." The story featured a picture of Hitler shaking hands with a little girl; the caption read "Hitler the Friend of Children." The Fuehrer was also fearless in his determination to carry out his mission, having flown "through snow and hailstorm in [a] flight to Frankfurt" in order to give a speech.[51]

The Nazis presented no coherent political platform. Hitler was their program. A full-page advertisement in the 4 April edition, for example, appealed to women. Only Hitler could provide food for their babies, and under his leadership, mothers would no longer have to work to feed their children. The 5 April issue contained a piece called "Adolf Hitler: My Program." As president, Hitler would end the "Germany of Parties" and replace it with the "Germany of the People." He promised to eliminate unemployment and inflation and would do so by annihilating the system which was the root of these ills.[52]

Hitler, of course, lost the second election as well. On 10 April he received 13.4 million votes (863,621 in Berlin, moving him up to second) while Hindenburg got 19.4 million

(1,328,941 in the capital city). Thaelmann received 3.7 million votes overall, 573,099 of them in Berlin. While Hindenburg had gained 700,000 votes over March's results, Hitler had increased his support by 2,000,000, a tremendous showing for the Nazi leader and his party. *Der Angriff* cited this as further evidence of the inevitability of a Nazi victory.[53]

In spite of the fact that Hitler had lost the presidential election of 1932, the campaign did much to contribute to his coming to power in January of the following year. First, and most obviously, the campaign gave Goebbels an opportunity to present a positive image of his Fuehrer. Hitler was, so *Der Angriff* claimed, a lover of children, a struggler for the improvement of Germany's future, the man who would abrogate the Versailles Treaty and a leader who would bring down the hated system. In short, he was the solution to all of Germany's problems. The campaign contributed much to the creation of the Hitler myth.

In addition, Hitler's bid for president helped to undermine the stability of Weimar democracy by causing a rift between Hindenburg and Bruening. There were two results of the election that the incumbent resented. First, the aging field marshal took umbrage at the fact that he had had to look to left-wing and centrist support to secure reelection. As Hindenburg himself asked: "Who elected me then? The Socialists elected me, the Catholics elected me and the *Berlin Daily News* elected me. My people did not elect me." In addition, Hindenburg objected to the fact that Bruening had failed to secure his reelection on the first ballot as he had promised. Hindenburg's disappointment at the course of the presidential contest was a major factor in the fall of the Bruening government in May 1932. The resulting instability and the incompetence of Bruening's successor, Franz von Papen, contributed greatly to Nazism's success. For this reason, although Hitler lost the presidential contest of 1932, the Nazis benefited the most from the election. The campaign strategy pursued in *Der Angriff* played an important role in bringing this about.[54]

4

The SA and
Political Violence

Among the most dynamic and revolutionary organizations within the NSDAP was its paramilitary wing, the SA. This was the case on both the national and Gau levels. Propaganda work and political violence carried out by Nazi storm troopers played an important role in the rise of National Socialism in Berlin, and the pages of *Der Angriff* mirrored this fact. The paper regularly contained entire columns dedicated to SA activities and political violence. The prominence of political violence on the pages of *Der Angriff* was the result of the confrontational atmosphere in Berlin. The city was the political center of Germany, and frequent street clashes between various paramilitary groups were part of political life. Many other Nazi sheets, *Der Stuermer* for example, did not place such a strong emphasis upon physical clashes with the enemy. There were simply not as many Communists in Nuremberg to fight. Thus, *Der Angriff's* attitudes stressing political violence serve as an example of how regional party leaders adapted their propaganda to local conditions. The ways in which Goebbels's newspaper portrayed the milieu of SA men also say much about the Nazi world view and how political propaganda reflected it.[1]

Although no one has done a quantitative analysis of the Berlin SA, there is enough information available to come to some tentative conclusions concerning its composition. Nazi sources record the number of SA men in the Berlin-Brandenburg district. In 1926, there were only 450 storm troopers in Berlin. By the time of the prohibition in May 1927, there were 800 SA men in the German capital. At the beginning of 1930, largely as a result of the unemployment caused by the world-wide depression, there were 3,000 storm troopers in the Berlin-Brandenburg SA, organized into 37 storms. In March 1931 there were 5,000 storm troopers comprising 100 *Stuerme*. The number of storm troopers in the Berlin-Brandenburg district of the SA continued to grow throughout the Weimar years, reaching 32,000 on the eve of the seizure of power.[2]

There are no sources available concerning the class and age composition of the Berlin-Brandenburg SA. There is, however, no reason to believe that they differ from nationwide statistics. According to Michael Kater, 72.6 percent of storm troopers in his sample were either workers or artisans. This is significantly higher than the percentage of party members who were from these same groups (32.1 percent). SA men were also young, 77.6 percent being under the age of thirty and 94.2 percent younger than forty-five. It is therefore safe to conclude that the Berlin SA was comprised primarily of young men from a working-class background.[3]

The motivations these men had for joining the SA were, to a large extent, the products of socioeconomic conditions. The number of storm troopers increased dramatically after the economic collapse of 1929-1930. There were a variety of reasons for this correlation. First, it is clear that the vast majority of storm troopers—estimates run as high as 70 percent—were jobless and most of the rest were underemployed. They turned to the SA as an alternative to employment. The organization saw to it that they had a place to stay and something to eat. Hostels (SA *Heime*) were established that provided unmarried, out-of-work storm troopers with the necessities of life. Also, vagrancy led to boredom and the SA provided disillusioned young men with a sense of purpose, a feeling of belonging to an organization in which they were appreciated. Disillusionment led to political violence. The prospect of violent confrontations with other paramilitary groups attracted many frustrated young men seeking an outlet. They were political soldiers fighting to destroy the republic that was responsible for their plight. Many would give their lives in pursuit of this nihilistic goal.[4]

The pages of *Der Angriff* reflected these harsh realities. The storm troopers depicted in Schweitzer's political cartoons were always young and muscular, identical in appearance—except for the Nazi armband—to the archetypical worker. They, like other members of Berlin's proletariat, had been disheartened by the defeat of 1918 and the actions of the inept democratic government. After losing their jobs, they felt unwanted but had found an organization that needed them, one that would feed them and give them a mission in life: saving Germany from the machinations of the Jews and democrats.[5]

Der Angriff presented SA men not only in a symbolic fashion but also as actual people. An article published in January 1931, for example, eulogized the martyred storm trooper, Ernst Schwartz. Schwartz was, the piece pointed out, "the son of a pastor, a soldier at the front, a painter, [and an] SA man." The article contained excerpts from some of his letters, relating how he had suffered in order to secure Germany's future. He had fought long and hard for his ideas, having been wounded in the First World War. After the war he suffered further as the "only" Nazi artist "in Berlin at that time." One of his major goals was to assure that the NSDAP supported the maintenance of "German art." Now this devout and committed man, a minister's son, was the victim of the Communists, who had brutally murdered him. The example of Schwartz, the editors of *Der Angriff* hoped, would contribute to the myth that storm troopers were ordinary men, making extraordinary sacrifices for the benefit of Germany.[6]

Among the indignities storm troopers had to accept was the possibility of being the "victims" of political violence. The world of the SA man was often a dangerous one, and a storm trooper had to be prepared to fight for his life at a moment's notice. He was the National Socialist "minute man." His opponents were most often the members of the other paramilitary organizations, the Communists' RFB and the SPD's Reichsbanner. Brawls among these groups—often leading to loss of life—were an integral part of the political landscape in Berlin, and *Der Angriff's* copy reflected this. In December 1930 and January 1931, for example, the paper published a series of articles providing boxing lessons to its readers.[7]

All stories concerned with politically motivated assaults insisted that the enemies of the storm troopers were to blame. The SA men were always, according to *Der Angriff*, the victims in any violent clash. The primary goal of Berlin's storm troopers was to carry out peacefully the tasks that the Gau leadership assigned them, whether distributing propaganda or marching through a working-class neighborhood. The Marxist parties, on the other hand, "practiced bloody terror and cowardly attacks."[8]

Standing behind these "cowardly attacks" were, of course, the Jews. The Jews benefited the most from these clashes between workers because they promoted division within the working-class community, which assured the continued domination of German society by the Jews. Indeed, members of the RFB and Reichsbanner were not really workers at all since they did the bidding of the Jews. Totally lacking in honor, these Marxist terrorists ambushed unsuspecting storm troopers in alleys, never attacking unless they had superior numbers. They were, according to *Der Angriff*, mere thugs, void of "human feelings." The paper attempted to dehumanize the enemy.[9]

Pubs and beer halls were often the sites of violent clashes. One of the first beer hall brawls reported in *Der Angriff* occurred in the Schlossbrauerei Schoeneberg in September 1927. The hall was crowded; nine hundred people were present, about one hundred of them Communists. During the course of the discussion, so the police report recounts, two Communists tried to receive permission to speak. When they could not produce Nazi party cards, permission was refused. A bloody brawl ensued. The Communists, singing the "Internationale," threw beer glasses and stools at Goebbels and the guest speaker, a man identified only as Haake. The fight spread outside, but the RFB men ran away when the police appeared on the scene. Nine people were arrested, eight Communists and one Nazi.[10]

Der Angriff reported the story briefly and, for the most part, accurately. There was, however, one important difference between the police and newspaper reports. *Der Angriff* insisted that the storm troopers present had forced the RFB men to retreat. The Communists were "driven out of the hall with bloody heads and [they] fled over roofs and into cellars." No mention of intervention by the police was made. Rather, the brave SA men present came to the rescue of their leaders, driving off the enemy and emerging, as always, victorious.[11]

Der Angriff's account of this beer hall battle in Schoeneberg evidences several propaganda techniques of the paper. First, and most important, the editors tried to base their copy, however loosely, upon the truth. A complete fabrication of events would be detected by those who were present and would serve to discredit the newspaper, which would be counterproductive, causing people not to take *Der Angriff's* copy seriously. In contrast, a carefully edited account of actual events could place the NSDAP in a positive light. In the Schoeneberg case, the KPD had initiated events, with the RFB men being the first to throw beer glasses and stools. The NSDAP could, to a certain extent, legitimately claim to have been the victims of red aggression. A foundation, however tenuous, in actual events contributed to the newspaper's credibility.

On the other hand, *Der Angriff* never published the truth when it would be disadvantageous to do so. The newspaper contended, for example, that the Nazis had driven the Communists from the Schlossbrauerei. The editors of the paper did this for two reasons. First, their version of events made it appear as if the NSDAP had emerged unscathed and victorious from an unprovoked attack. Second, it would have been unwise to admit that the police had frightened away the RFB, which would have implied that the NSDAP needed the police to fight its battles. It would suggest that Goebbels and his followers were helpless in the face of the "red horde," something *Der Angriff* could never admit. In addition, the paper consistently claimed that the Berlin Police Force was a tool of the system, the handmaid of the Jews and the parties of the left. It could not admit that the police would protect the Nazis. Lying, or neglecting to relate completely the course of events, was a popular ploy that contributed greatly to the propaganda mission of *Der Angriff*. Berlin's storm troopers surely appreciated this propaganda technique.[12]

The ultimate sacrifice any SA man could make was to die for his ignoble cause. This happened frequently. By the summer of 1932, about 350 storm troopers had been killed throughout the Reich, seventeen of them in Berlin between 1926 and August 1932. These "martyrs," having made the ultimate sacrifice for the movement, became Christ figures in Nazi mythology, the "holy sacrifice" Germany had made at the altar of the Elders of Zion. The NSDAP lauded them in song and poetry. The poem "Two Hundred Are Dead," published in *Der Angriff* in January 1931, is an excellent example of Nazi martyrology.

> They fought by day and in dark night,
> They have buried two hundred comrades,
> Have mourned but never taken flight,
> And have struggled and only said one thing is right:
> Two hundred are dead, but hundreds of thousands stand,
> Because Germany must not fall or be ruined they demand
> They have fought for the new, the approaching state,
> They stand together despite terror, death and hate,
> They keep the flame and will not let it flee
> And hold it tightly until Germany is great and free.
> Two hundred are dead, so the rippling flags wave
> Because Germany must not fall or be lost to the brave.[13]

The first storm trooper killed in Berlin after *Der Angriff* began publication in 1927 was Walter Fischer, a member of *Sturm* 13. Communists shot him on the evening of 14 December 1929 in Wilmersdorf. The nineteen-year-old Fischer, according to the Nazi version of the story, was on his way to a pub after an SA meeting. Along with several of his comrades, he wanted to end the day with a beer at *Sturm* 13's tavern, "Unger." Rumors claiming that armed RFB men from the pub "Lauenburger" were roaming the streets around Wegenerstrasse spread among the tavern's patrons, though Fischer and his comrades were unaware of the danger. To make matters worse, the SA men in this district had no weapons with which to defend themselves; the police had confiscated them earlier that day. Because the Communists had destroyed many of the surrounding streetlights, the neighborhood was dark. Shots rang out. Fischer was hit in the shoulder. He was taken to the hospital, where he died later that night.[14]

Presented with its first SA martyr, *Der Angriff* was determined to benefit from his death. The 19 December issue of the paper contained a front-page story, written by Lippert, which paid tribute to the fallen storm trooper. Fischer was, Lippert charged, the victim of a hypocritical system that espoused "humanitarianism" and "pacifism." But Weimar authorities only paid lip service to these views because they permitted young men to be gunned down in the street. And the system would do nothing. This problem, the article continued, was not confined to the city of Berlin. Every day, throughout Germany, fifty storm troopers were attacked; and the government did nothing. Rather, the police merely blamed the violence upon the victims, calling them "political rowdies" unworthy of protection. Therefore, the SA had to defend itself.[15]

Lippert then turned to an attack upon the Weimar constitution, which defended Communist murderers of unsuspecting SA men. A document that would protect assassins was not worthy of Germany and should be abrogated for the benefit of the entire nation. If this were not done, Germany could be certain that men such as those who ambushed Fischer would come to rule the country. The constitution protected no one but the guilty, those who murdered innocent men like Fischer.[16]

Fischer was the first storm trooper martyred during the period 1927-1933 but by no means the most important in Nazi propaganda. Horst Wessel, who died in February 1930 after a five-week battle for life, became the most prominent figure in the martyrology of the SA. The death of Wessel, the leader of Storm 5, became the subject of poems, books, and even a movie, "Hans Westmar." "The Horst Wessel Song"

("Die Fahne hoch") became the official ballad of the NSDAP. *Der Angriff* played no small role in creating what historian Jay Baird has called "the myth of resurrection and return" surrounding Wessel's death.[17]

Wessel's background was useful in creating this myth. The son of a Lutheran pastor, he would be just twenty-two years old when he died. The year 1926 saw him begin to study law at the University of Berlin. The pretentious intellectual atmosphere at the university repelled him, and he joined the SA in December of the same year. Wessel soon became famous for his impassioned speeches calling for the liberation of Germany, making him popular with the other storm troopers. His speaking ability, coupled with intense popularity, led to his appointment as leader of Storm 5 in 1929. Wessel soon got a reputation in Berlin's proletarian districts as a good organizer and propagandist for the NSDAP, which contributed to the decision to murder him in January 1930.[18]

The events surrounding Wessel's death are somewhat unclear. Because of effective KPD propaganda surrounding his murder—*Rote Fahne* insisted that Wessel was shot because he was a pimp—it is traditionally argued that Wessel was killed in a disagreement over a woman. In September 1929, he moved in with his girlfriend, the prostitute Erna Jaenicke, who lived in Friedrichshain. The Communist Ali Hoehler supposedly shot Wessel on 14 January 1930 in a dispute concerning Jaenicke's services.[19]

Baird has determined, however, that Jaenicke's affections had nothing to do with Wessel's murder. Rather, the storm leader was having some difficulties with his landlady, Frau Salm, because he and Jaenicke were living together. Further, Salm did not like the noise made during the SA meetings frequently held in Wessel's apartment. She turned to the local RFB section, headquartered in the tavern "Der Baer," for aid. Hoehler, because of Wessel's reputation among Berlin's proletariat, was willing to deal with the storm leader. On 14 January, Hoehler and several comrades burst into the apartment, shouted "You know what this is for," and shot Wessel. As Baird points out, treatment was delayed because of a refusal to secure the services of a nearby Jewish doctor. Wessel was taken to the Friedrichshain Hospital, where he died on 23 February 1930.[20]

Der Angriff began to create a legend concerning Wessel even before the *Sturmfuehrer's* demise. An article appearing on 19 January lauded the dying storm trooper. He was attacked, the paper argued, because he was "the most active storm leader of Berlin;" so the Communists, who could not match Wessel's dedication and enthusiasm, shot him. Wessel had assumed control of SA Troop 34, headquartered in the heart of "red Friedrichshain," and had turned it into a *Sturm*. He was able to succeed in the heart of Communist territory because he, unlike the KPD, understood the "soul of the proletariat." The leader of Storm 5 saw every German as his "brother and comrade." *Der Angriff*, countering Communist propaganda, insisted that for these "purely political" reasons, Communists had assaulted Wessel. Further, not only was the KPD guilty of the attack on Wessel, but so was the system. Hoehler had recently been arrested for assault but had conveniently been broken out of jail. The implication was that, as usually was the case, the system had managed to protect the guilty rather than the innocent. To make matters worse, *Der Angriff* recorded, Hoehler would never suffer for his crime, for the KPD leadership had spirited him away to his comrades in the Soviet Union.[21]

Another article in *Der Angriff*, written by Goebbels, began by depicting the "deathwatch" over Wessel. Concerned comrades and candles and flowers surrounded the wounded storm trooper. "On the wall hangs a picture of [Wessel's] father in [his] vestments." The room was blanketed in silence, onlookers weeping quietly. Horst Wessel was "fighting . . . his hardest battle: that against death." In spite of his condition— he could neither eat nor drink—Wessel looked forward to visits from his comrades. "This young man has lost two liters of blood." He was conscious throughout the ordeal, and, in spite of the pain, had not so much as whimpered. Wessel kept his spirits up as always. The storm leader suddenly began to speak. "We must endure!" he said. "We are still needed," he

Heilige Opfer

Wenn es noch eine Gerechtigkeit gibt — — die Vergeltung muß kommen!

"Holy Offerings. If there is to be justice—retribution must come."

continued. "I am happy!" Wessel, in spite of his pain, kept the movement foremost in his thoughts. The Gauleiter gave Wessel his hand but could no longer contain his grief and had to leave. Goebbels "would never forget" this moment. The murderers must be punished, he insisted.[22]

Der Angriff also began to use Christian motifs in the creation of the Horst Wessel myth. A cartoon appearing in the 23 January edition depicted the "Holy sacrifices" of the Berlin NSDAP. On the ground were the bodies of several martyred storm troopers, Walther Fischer and Wessel (who was not yet dead) among them. Standing over the bodies was an RFB man holding a pistol. Behind him, standing in front of the masthead of the *Rote Fahne*, was "the Jewish murderer," the RFB man his willing "tool." The caption read: "If there is to be justice—retribution must come."[23]

After Wessel's death, *Der Angriff* grafted another Christian theme onto the Wessel myth: the concept of victory in death. The storm trooper was not really dead at all because his memory would live on in the hearts and minds of the comrades he left behind. He provided inspiration that would cause others to take up his cause. The RFB, which was responsible for his murder, would have to look upon the SA with new respect and fear because the death of Horst Wessel would provide new strength and determination for Marxism's enemies. In short, Wessel had not died in vain; he had helped to assure that the movement, Germany, would live.[24]

The theme of heroic death remained an important one for *Der Angriff* throughout the rest of the "years of struggle." Among those added to the pantheon of Nazi martyrs during this period was storm trooper Ernst Schwartz. Schwartz was attending an SA meeting in the tavern "Bergschloss" in Frohnau on the evening of 19 January 1932. While walking home through Reinickendorf with his comrades from Storm 4, Schwartz became involved in a pitched street battle with Communists who attacked the storm troopers outside the collection of wooden hovels known as "Felseneck." During the course of the fight, shots were fired from one of the nearby shacks. The Communists brandished knives. Schwartz was killed, stabbed in the heart. A Communist also died during the skirmish. Two others, both Nazis, were severely wounded in the course of the battle.[25]

Goebbels and the staff of *Der Angriff* had yet another opportunity to reap benefit from the death of a storm trooper. The paper held that Schwartz must not die in vain. His noble demise must inspire others to make the ultimate sacrifice for their country and the movement. They must be willing to go "from graveside to [a] new struggle." His comrades must avenge his death, thereby seeking the salvation of Germany. This would give meaning to Schwartz's life of struggle and his noble death.[26]

Der Angriff contended that, when the RFB murdered SA men, it was carrying out a conscious plan. The paper used the murder of Schwartz to bring this point home. The Communists held that the working-class neighborhoods were their turf and became determined to end Nazi penetration of these areas. In this case, the plan began with a series of circulars posted in the Felseneck district. These *Flugblaetter* called for establishment of a "unified front against fascism," insisting that the Nazis should not be permitted to enter the area. To complement the distribution of propaganda, the local Communists began to attack small groups of Nazis, on one occasion assaulting a distributor of *Der Angriff* in the hallway of an apartment building.[27]

Having contributed to this atmosphere of hate, it was just a matter of time until the KPD's efforts came to fruition. On the night of the murder, Communist troops patrolled the streets of Reineckendorf, looking for trouble. Local police, aware of the tense situation in the area, were also on alert. As Schwartz and his men approached, they were ambushed by inhabitants of the surrounding shacks. The Communists had obviously been waiting for the members of Troop III of Storm 4, murder in their hearts. Schwartz, somewhat streetwise, tried to get his men out of the situation, but Communists cut off all paths of retreat. Three hundred shots were fired at the storm troopers. While policemen watched, the leader of Troop III was stabbed by a "red murderer." Such events were clearly the result of a conspiracy aimed at the murder of a local SA leader. These street clashes were not the products of coincidence, but part of a conscious policy on the part of the KPD to drive the NSDAP out of the working-class neighborhoods. The Reds, however, would ultimately fail.[28]

Storm troopers were not the only victims of red campaigns to take over the streets. On 24 January 1932, a gang of Communists murdered the Hitler Youth Herbert Norkus in Moabit. Like Horst Wessel, Norkus would become one of the most important figures in National Socialist propaganda, and, once again, *Der Angriff* played an important role in securing his place in Nazi mythology.[29]

On 24 January 1932, the fifteen-year-old Norkus was placing flyers in mailboxes in Moabit, accompanied by a comrade, Johannes Kirsch. As they left the fourth house on Gotzkowskistrasse, they saw thirty-five to forty Communists. The Hitler Youths, keeping on the watch for danger, continued to distribute flyers. As they approached one of the houses, they discovered that the Communists were behind them. One of the "reds" told them to "stand still." When Kirsch tried to place a flyer in the door of the house, one of the RFB men hit him in the back. Kirsch managed to escape harm by hiding behind a trash can. Norkus, however, was not as fortunate.[30]

Norkus tried to flee down Gotzkowskistrasse, turning onto Zwinglistrasse. After he unsuccessfully attempted to gain sanctuary in a nearby building, his enemies caught him. Although they knocked him down, he managed to escape once again, trying to seek refuge in the Kirschner school. His failure to do so enabled the Communists to fall upon him again, this time stabbing him. Norkus, somehow succeeding in escaping yet again, managed to get help from the proprietor of a cleaning establishment. He was taken to the hospital, where he died.[31]

The following day, *Der Angriff* carried news of "the assassination of the Hitler Youth." On Sunday morning, the paper recorded, Norkus and his comrades were peacefully distributing leaflets announcing a Hitler Youth function. While they were doing so, a "terror troop" of the RFB, acting on a tip from its network of "bicyclists and other couriers," made plans to attack the unsuspecting adolescents. The Communists waited for Norkus and Kirsch in a "dark corner." They fell upon the greatly outnumbered Hitler Youths, and in the course of events "knives flashed," and Norkus received "numerous stab wounds." Once again, the Nazis were the victims of a planned Communist assault. A more detailed story in the same edition numbered Norkus's attackers at forty and his stab wounds at six.[32]

Another piece in *Der Angriff* discussed the "men behind the cowardly assassination": "International Workers' Aid, Red Aid and [the] Leadership of the KPD." The killers of Norkus were not the only people guilty of his death. Also bearing responsibility for the deed was the leadership of the KPD, which had organized a systematic terror campaign against Berlin's Nazis. The leaders of the Berlin government, the hated system, were also held accountable for Norkus's murder. They had refused to put an end to the red terror. The police, who were so adept at solving nonpolitical murders, almost never captured the culprits who murdered a Nazi. The reason was simple: they did not want to pursue these cases tenaciously. This, in the eyes of *Der Angriff*, was further evidence of the bankruptcy of the Weimar government.[33]

Norkus had become yet another martyr for the Nazi cause. He had, *Der Angriff* claimed, answered the call of the chief of the Hitler Youth to help propagate the ideas of his Fuehrer, to win Germany's youth for the coming Third Reich. Norkus knew that he might very well have to sacrifice his life for the movement, but, even though he was not yet a man, he understood that his mission was more important than his own existence. Norkus, who had grown up in the shadow of red oppression, went willingly into enemy territory and fell there, contending that "Germany should live, even if we must die."[34]

Yet Norkus had not really died. In a front-page story in *Der Angriff*, Goebbels recorded the Hitler Youth's resurrection:

There in the bleak, gray twilight, yellowed, tortured eyes stare into the emptiness. His tender head has been trampled into a bloody pulp. Long, deep wounds extend down the slender body, and a deadly laceration tears through his lungs and heart. . . . Yet it is as if life stirs anew out of pale death. Look now, the slender, elegant body begins to move. Slowly, slowly he rises as if conjured up by magic, until he stands tall in all his youthful glory right before my trembling eyes. And without moving his lips, a frail child's voice is heard as if speaking from all eternity: "They killed me. They plunged the murderers's daggers into my breast and mangled my head. . . . This happened only because I—still a child—wanted to serve my country. . . . *I am Germany* . . . one of you millions. . . . What is mortal in me will perish. But my spirit, which is immortal, will remain with you. And it . . . will show you the way. Until the Reich comes."[35]

Norkus was not dead. He lived as long as other Germans pursued his vision. The dead Hitler Youth would serve as an inspiration to millions.

There are several themes that run throughout *Der Angriff's* propaganda concerning political violence. They say much about the way in which the leadership of the Berlin NSDAP viewed the movement and how most effectively to spread its message. Studying these motifs will aid in the understanding of National Socialism and, more specifically, its propaganda.

First, *Der Angriff* always depicted Nazis involved in political violence as victims. Nazis never initiated a confrontation and were always the prey of Marxists and Jews. In each case discussed above, the Nazis attacked were, in the view of *Der Angriff*, engaged in peaceful activity, such as distributing propaganda leaflets or merely walking home to their families after an evening at the local storm pub. In short, the goal of National Socialism was not violence, but merely the salvation of Germany. Others, who objected to this goal, felt compelled to destroy Nazism violently because they could not defeat it through peaceful methods. The Marxists, no better than animals, did this consciously.

Der Angriff also had much to say about Nazi victims of political violence. They were ordinary people who found themselves in extraordinary circumstances and rose to the occasion. Horst Wessel, for example, had not intended to martyr himself for his cause. In the end, however, he was willing to do so if it came to that. Germany, not his own welfare, was his primary interest. Even on his deathbed, Wessel's foremost concern was the success of the movement. Those who remembered him, *Der Angriff* contended, would do him a great service by continuing his mission.

The paper consistently used Christian themes in portraying Nazi martyrs. They had died not to destroy Germany but to save it. They were "holy sacrifices." A storm trooper, like Christ, died so that others might live. Herbert Norkus, Goebbels implied, had risen from the dead so that others would continue his mission. As long as their ideas lived, these men would not truly be dead.

These themes were powerful propaganda weapons. They depicted Nazism as a dynamic movement. People were willing to make the ultimate sacrifice for its ideas. To espouse Nazism was, therefore, by implication to adopt a noble cause.

No one would willingly fight and die for anything less. *Der Angriff* hoped to attract and keep supporters by stressing these themes, and stories concerning martyrs to the Nazi cause provided a valuable foundation upon which these motifs could be constructed.

Der Angriff's involvement with Nazi paramilitary politics went beyond merely recording the exploits of SA men. The paper often found itself entangled in the internal politics of the paramilitary group. One such occasion was the revolt of the eastern SA in April 1931. This rebellion is of interest not only because *Der Angriff* played an important role, but also because of the part its editor, Goebbels, played in the revolt.[36]

The Gauleiter's actions are of interest because he was the Nazi leader at the center of the conflagration, Berlin. Further, he almost lost his position as leader of the Gau and its newspaper because he seemingly could not control the SA in his region. Also, Walther Stennes, the leader of the rebels, claimed that Goebbels was intimately involved in the April action. Finally, the Berlin Police, which had an informant in the Stennes camp, claimed that the Gauleiter fled to Munich and told Hitler about the SA leader's plans, thereby betraying Stennes and helping to crush the revolt.[37]

Fortunately, the recent appearance of previously unpublished entries from the Gauleiter's diaries make it possible to trace his actions. Goebbels's personal account, coupled with other evidence, makes it clear that the situation was much more complicated than the police believed. Although the April 1931 rebellion is of primary concern here, a brief recounting of the August-September 1930 revolt is necessary for understanding the issues facing the Berlin party leader.

The catalyst for the August uprising was a disagreement between Hitler and the Supreme Commander of the SA (Osaf), Franz Pfeffer. The issue was the position of SA representatives on the NSDAP Reichstag list for the upcoming election. At a leadership conference held on 2-3 August 1930, Pfeffer demanded that storm troopers receive three secure places. Hitler refused because of a growing disagreement between the party and the paramilitary leadership. Pfeffer saw the SA as a military organization that would play an active role in the violent overthrow of the Weimar government. In contrast, Hitler, who had committed himself to a "legal" seizure of power, saw the SA's function as primarily political. Its members were to carry out propaganda work and serve as guards at party rallies, although occasional clashes with the Communists aided in creating an image of the NSDAP as a bulwark of law and order. Because of his views on the role of the SA, Hitler wanted the organization subordinate to the party, a position Pfeffer would not accept. On 12 August Pfeffer resigned, effective 1 September.[38]

Because of repeated clashes with the RFB, the Osaf's position had gained preeminence in Berlin. Hence, the reaction to Pfeffer's resignation was strongest in the capital. The Berlin SA went on strike, refusing to distribute propaganda or defend rallies until Hitler reinstated Pfeffer. The leader of the mutiny was the supreme commander of the SA for eastern Germany (Osaf-ost), Walther Stennes. The Osaf-ost had been a right-wing revolutionary since leading troops in the aborted putsch by the "Black Reichswehr" (troops assembled by right-wing groups in violation of the Versailles Treaty) in 1923. By 1927, his reputation within *voelkisch* paramilitary circles had led to his appointment as Osaf-ost. Because of his background, Stennes was a strong supporter of Pfeffer and would not watch his superior ousted without a fight.[39]

Under Stennes's leadership the strike spread. At the end of August, Goebbels received word that the strikers would present the party with an ultimatum concerning the Reichstag list. He faced an all-out rebellion of the forces under the Osaf-ost. The demands of the strikers increased, Stennes insisting that the party do more to help unemployed members of the SA. Hitler and the other party "big shots" (*Bonzen*) had, Stennes alleged, abandoned their socialist goals in order to gain the support of big business, thereby selling out hungry storm troopers and their families.[40]

When Hitler refused to meet Stennes's demands, SA Storm 31 seized the Berlin party headquarters and the offices of *Der Angriff*, injuring two SS guards. Hitler's response was effective and quick. He personally assumed the position vacated by Pfeffer and went to Berlin, where he used his immense popularity to quell the rebellion. The Fuehrer visited SA pubs on 1 September, assuring those assembled that he was concerned with their welfare. All present swore an oath of loyalty to Hitler, who ordered that twenty pfennigs be added to party dues to help the beleaguered SA. Goebbels then spoke, echoing Hitler's promises. While Goebbels hoped that the episode was closed, it was clear that the fundamental issue, the proper role of the SA, remained unresolved. Also, the strong "social-revolutionary component" within the SA had come to the fore.[41]

The revolt also presented the Berlin Gauleiter with a serious problem. He enjoyed the privilege of being leader of both the party and SA within his region. In other Gaue, the leader of the SA reported directly to the Osaf for the area. In Berlin he was responsible to the Gauleiter, who could lose this power if the SA were to revolt again. Another rebellion would prove that Goebbels was unworthy of the authority given him by his leader. He therefore had to be sure to maintain the dominance of the party over the paramilitary group. On the other hand, Stennes was very popular with the rank and file of the Berlin SA, and Goebbels could not afford to alienate him; this could cause another mutiny.[42]

Realizing his predicament, Goebbels began to court Stennes's favor, meeting frequently with the SA leader. One such occasion was 20 September 1930, when an SA gathering brought them together. They spoke until two in the morning. In his diary, the Gauleiter recorded that he felt Stennes was a man with whom he could work. Another important meeting occurred in the Gauleiter's home on 11 January 1931, during which Goebbels and Stennes discussed the problems existing between the SA and SS, which was becoming elitist and increasingly independent of the SA. Stennes opposed this trend, and Goebbels echoed his concern. "Stennes appears to want peace with me," Goebbels recorded in his diary. They were "becoming much closer" and the SA leader could serve as "something of a counterweight against Munich."[43]

At the same time that the Gauleiter tried to win the trust of the SA, he complained about the trouble it gave him. Knowing that the issues raised in August were unresolved, he recorded in his diary that "I also do not believe that Stennes will give [us] peace in the long run." The following month, Goebbels lamented that Hitler was trying to increase the powers of the national SA leadership, thereby undermining Stennes's strength. He feared problems would arise from the "many utopian romantics" who stood behind the Osaf-ost. In the end, he was sure that the issues raised in the late summer of 1930 remained unresolved.[44]

While Goebbels tried to seize control of the political situation, the SA felt itself increasingly alienated from the party leadership. Ernst Roehm, whom Hitler named Osaf in January 1931, reorganized the SA in the eastern districts, thereby taking control of the SA in Silesia from Stennes. Hitler also issued a decree on 20 February which made the SA subordinate to the party organization at the Gau level. Both of these moves were designed to decrease the power of the Osaf-ost and his supporters.[45]

Stennes's reaction was swift but cautious. On the last day of February 1931, he composed a letter to Roehm in which he voiced his concerns about recent developments, protesting the party's abrogation of the traditional rights of local SA leaders. Instead of undermining the authority of the organization's leadership, the party should deal with matters of immediate importance, especially the economic plight of unemployed SA men.[46]

In the meantime, the situation became more uncomfortable for Goebbels. On 15 March he spoke with Hermann Goering who scolded him for being too close to Stennes. Unnamed party leaders had made accusations questioning Goebbels's loyalty. Goebbels and Goering argued about the new party program, the Gauleiter maintaining that it had renounced socialism. "*Armer Sozialismus!*" he lamented. Later that same day, Goebbels told Willi Hess, an assistant to the Gauleiter of Duesseldorf, that the Fuehrer was oblivious to the views of the masses. "Next time [I see him] I'll talk turkey with him [*bei ihm Fraktur reden*]" about this.[47]

Goebbels soon got his chance to do so, but not under conditions he liked. On the evening of 30 March, he met with Bruno Wetzel, the leader of the Berlin SA and a strong supporter of Stennes. According to one account, the Gauleiter promised Wetzel that he would "fight on Stennes's side" in any effort to establish an independent revolutionary movement in northern Germany. Then, so this police account goes, Goebbels, realizing that another SA mutiny was afoot, fled to Munich to tell Hitler about it. The Gauleiter hoped that this action would help him maintain his post after the rebellion was over.[48]

Wilhelm Jahn, an SA squad leader, gave a somewhat different version of the gathering. Goebbels, holding that the Berlin SA was right to resent the policies of Munich, vowed never to take action against Wetzel and always to fight by his side. The Berlin Gauleiter emphasized, however, that the time had not yet come for a reckoning with Munich. Goebbels made only cryptic references to the meeting in his diary, merely stating that the situation in the SA was a cause for concern and that trouble was likely. He had, however, made no concrete agreement and, once again, kept his options open.[49]

The Gauleiter's actions support the Jahn account. He did not run away to Munich; Hitler called him to a conference in Weimar. On his way, he stopped in Dresden, where he gave two speeches before proceeding. Had Goebbels known about the impending revolt and had he wanted to inform Hitler, he would probably have gone directly to the Fuehrer. If, on the other hand, he planned to participate in the rebellion, he would not have gone to meet with the party boss at all. Further, a successful SA revolt would only decrease the Gauleiter's power because it would clearly make Stennes the number one man in Berlin. Goebbels was unlikely to support such an outcome. It is most likely, therefore, that, while he suspected that another SA revolt was likely, he did not know when. Supporting this interpretation is the fact that, after the mutiny began, Stennes sent a delegation to Weimar to win the support of Goebbels, who had, by then, gone to Munich with Hitler. This would have been unlikely had Goebbels known about the rebellion in advance. On the other hand, this also makes it clear that, because of his actions in Berlin, Stennes expected Goebbels to support him. Goebbels had considered one day turning against Hitler. This is evinced by a diary entry made shortly after he learned of the rebellion: "For me there is no longer any question, I will remain loyal to Hitler." The Gauleiter knew that his contacts with the SA would cause him serious difficulties, confessing that "there remains nothing for me to do but conceal the facts."[50]

Goebbels learned about what happened from Roehm. Hitler had removed Stennes, who refused to accept his dismissal and rebelled during the night of 31 March-1 April. Once again, the SA stormed the Berlin party headquarters and the offices of *Der Angriff*. With the aid of the managing editor, Weissauer, pro-Stennes editions of the newspaper appeared on the first two days of April. Upon learning that he would not support them, the insurgents deposed Goebbels and named Wetzel the new Gauleiter. Hitler gave Daluege, who by now was the leader of the Berlin SS, responsibility for crushing the rebellion.[51]

This would prove more problematic than in the previous summer. Unlike September, the revolt spread throughout eastern Germany. Of the 25,000 men in Stennes's Group East, 8,000-10,000 joined the rebellion. The Berlin Police estimated the breakdown as 1,500 in Berlin, 2,000 in Brandenburg, 3,000 in Silesia (an area not under Stennes's jurisdiction at the start of the revolt), and 2,000 in Pomerania.[52]

The motives of the mutineers were largely the same as in September. The party had allegedly forgotten the plight of the economically downtrodden SA and betrayed the storm troopers to gain the support of big business. Hitler had removed Stennes because the SA leader had the courage to fight for his men against the party organization, run by "bourgeois liberals." The insurgents demanded that the legal course must be abandoned, because "the path to the people's community [*Volksgemeinschaft*] means struggle and not peace and order [i.e., democracy]."[53]

The result of the revolt was a schism in the SA. After

surrendering party headquarters, Stennes formed the Nationalsozialistische Kampfbewegung Deutschlands (National
Socialist Movement for Germany's Struggle) or NSKD. He
maintained earlier contacts with the KPD, which found the
revolutionary zeal of the NSKD attractive and hoped to ab-
sorb the group, and eventually formed an alliance with Otto
Strasser's Kampfgemeinschaft. This was a natural outcome
of the similarities between the programs of the two groups.
In May the NSKD had 6,000 members, 500 of them in Berlin.
Throughout the rest of the year and into the next, it continued to lose members to both the KPD and NSDAP and gradually faded from the political scene.[54]

Although the mutiny did not cause serious problems for
the Nazis in the long run, it caused difficulties for Goebbels so
severe that they affected his health. The SA in his Gau had
rebelled twice within several months, raising serious doubts
concerning his leadership. Several leading Nazis, most impor-
tantly Goering, accused Goebbels of incompetence. To make
matters worse, Stennes claimed that Goebbels had participated in the planning of the revolt. Hence, the Berlin Police
expected him to be replaced as soon as the crisis subsided.[55]

Realizing that he faced a "great personal test," Goebbels
remained close to the man upon whom all his political fortunes depended, Hitler. He did everything possible to assure
the Fuehrer of his loyalty. Hitler, seeing that the brilliant propagandist was an invaluable asset, stood by Goebbels. On 3
April, the Nazi leader published an open letter to the Berlin
Gauleiter in the party newspaper. Hitler began by recounting
the conditions under which Goebbels assumed the helm in
the capital. The Gauleiter had built the movement in Berlin
from the ground up. Hitler thanked him for his "unswerving
loyalty to the movement and to me personally as Fuehrer."[56]

Goebbels, however, did not go unpunished. Because of the
role *Der Angriff* had played in the rebellion, he temporarily lost
managerial control of the paper. Hitler dispatched Amann,
manager of the party publishing company, to Berlin to take
the financial reins of the organ. Goebbels, however, maintained editorship of *Der Angriff*. While it soon became clear

that Amann did not control the daily operation of the news-paper, he did force the Gauleiter temporarily to reduce its length from twelve to ten pages. Also, several staff members, most prominently Weissauer, were purged from the party. Goebbels successfully resisted efforts on the part of Amann and Hans Hinkel, Amann's assistant, to take over *Der Angriff* for the national organization. The proposal called for Hinkel to assume permanent managerial control of the paper while Goebbels kept the editorship. How the Gauleiter accomplished this is unclear, but, on 19 June, Amann returned to Munich and things returned to normal in the offices of *Der Angriff*.[57]

Not only did Goebbels successfully resist efforts to seize control of his newspaper, but he also fought to maintain his regional leadership. As events progressed and Stennes made accusations concerning the Gauleiter's part in the uprising, an increasing number of Nazi leaders became convinced that he must be fired. Goebbels considered the possibilities of leaving the country for six months or serving some of the jail sentences he had accrued for his political activities and re-turning when things quieted down. A meeting with his chief on 27 April changed the situation. Hitler told Goebbels that he trusted him and that "Berlin belongs to you and so should it remain!"[58]

Goebbels did not limit his efforts to meetings with the Fuehrer. He cultivated good relations with the man who re-placed Stennes as Osaf-ost, Paul Schulz. He also published articles in *Der Angriff* claiming that Stennes was a liar and police spy. Speeches to packed houses showed both the local party membership and the national leadership that he was indispensable to the movement. On 16 April 1931, Goebbels spoke to 4,000 SA men in the Sportpalast. As he recounted the tribulations the party had recently endured, many in the au-dience wept. He later recorded in his diary that "no devil would ever take these young men away from me again." This was true; the 27 April meeting with Hitler had made it clear that he had weathered the storm.[59]

The facts surrounding Goebbels's actions during this period indicate something about the character of the publisher of *Der Angriff*. His primary goal was power, and he always did what was necessary to obtain and keep it. Goebbels wooed Stennes in order to keep the SA leader contented, but when Stennes threatened his authority, he turned contritely to Hitler. He simply was not willing to risk his positions as Gauleiter and editor of *Der Angriff* to benefit his greatest political rival, Walther Stennes.

Goebbels's part in the second SA mutiny also shows something about Nazi intra-party politics. Clearly, the NSDAP was not monolithic; at least two factions had developed. There were many within the party who wanted to abandon Hitler's call for a legal seizure of power. Others insisted upon the efficacy of the Fuehrer's course. The unfortunate Gauleiter found himself in a difficult situation because people within both camps plotted against him. When the situation got out of control, he turned to the Fuehrer, who was, in the end, the ultimate arbiter of power within the NSDAP. Having been granted Hitler's absolution, he could return to his post and serve his leader. The extent and limitations of Hitler's power are probably the most important lessons to be learned from Goebbels's and *Der Angriff's* roles in the Stennes Revolt.[60]

5

Appeals to the Proletariat

Berlin was a working-class city. Of its total population of about four million in 1922, around 956,000 (24 percent) were workers. There were around 25,000 businesses employing ten or more people, the German capital being a center of the metal, chemical, and clothing industries. Berlin was the most industrialized city on the European continent and the fourth most industrialized urban center in the world (trailing only London, New York, and Chicago).[1]

Because of the working-class origins of so much of Berlin's population, the two proletarian parties dominated politics in the city. During the period 1924-1933, the KPD and SPD together received anywhere from 41 to 57.6 percent of the vote in Reichstag elections. Support remained constant at over 54.3 percent after the 20 May 1928 Reichstag election. The most the Nazis ever polled was 28.6 percent in July 1932. Although these results belie Goebbels's claims to have "conquered" Berlin, they do mark a significant improvement over the 1.5 percent polled in May 1928.[2]

The social and political composition of Berlin's population presented serious difficulties to the editors of *Der Angriff*. Even after the party's supposed change of course in 1928—away from appeals to the proletariat in favor of attracting peasant support—the paper continued its mission to Berlin's working classes. Goebbels and his editors simply had no choice. If they ceased to appeal to the proletariat, they would be neglecting a significant group. This shows that the Nazi party had not given up completely on Germany's workers.

Attempts to win working-class support also call into question claims that National Socialism was ultimately an antimodernist movement. The proletariat, after all, is the most modern of social classes. Further, as was shown in chapter two, circumstantial evidence implies that a significant number of *Der Angriff's* readers were workers. Yet criticism of historians who approach Nazism as an antimodernist movement can be countered by the fact that, as evidence culled from *Der Angriff* will show, the Nazis tried to attract the support of workers with appeals to tradition.[3]

On the other hand, many of the propaganda techniques employed by *Der Angriff*, which were derivative of KPD and SPD methods, were modern in origin. Among these was the "proletarian novel," which the working-class parties had been publishing for years. From the inception of the paper—they only became a regular feature after the Berlin organ became a daily—the staff of *Der Angriff* made occasional use of serialized proletarian novels to emphasize Nazism's affinity for causes affecting Berlin's working classes. These stories graphically portrayed life in the proletarian districts of the German capital and suggested a cure for the ills that plagued the city's streets. The serials often recounted the conversion of the main character to National Socialism, indicating the path the reader should take to secure Germany's redemption.[4]

Among the serials to appear in the first year of *Der Angriff's* publication was "Hans Sturm's [Storm's] Awakening" by Otto Baugert. It is the story of a mechanic who becomes a Nazi after attending a rally in Berlin. The first installment begins with the unmarried Sturm, having received his pay for the previous week's labor, wondering what he should do during the upcoming weekend. He wanders the streets in search of entertainment. Baugert graphically depicts the dehumanizing milieu of the city. As Sturm travels through Berlin, he sees the light from the street lamps reflecting off the asphalt and hears the noise of the trollies, trucks and cars that drive by. He is clearly a man lost and unappreciated in all this activity.[5]

Suddenly, Sturm spots a "flaming red poster," reading "German Racial Comrades [*Volksgenossen*]! Men of the Fist and Brains!" It is a call to a political rally. At the bottom of the poster is a swastika. The young engineer has seen this symbol before. Although he has never attended an NSDAP rally, he knows, because of what his fellow workers have told him, that the Nazis are "bandits" and "killers of workers." In addition, they are reactionaries who want to return the Kaiser to power. In spite of these "prejudices," he is so bored that he decides to attend anyway.[6]

Sturm arrives at the meeting place fifteen minutes before the rally is to begin. He is surprised to discover that the assembly is to take place in a large hall that "seats a minimum of three thousand people." In spite of the size of the room there is no place to sit. Men are standing in the aisles, and several hundred are outside, hoping to gain admittance. Because of the crowd, the police close the doors at ten minutes to eight. "Things promise to become interesting." Looking about the room, he notices a flag. It is the "victorious and steady" swastika. "He feels: this symbol does not stand for mediocrity, weakness or idle talk; it demands fanatical support or fanatical hate!"[7]

Sturm then begins to observe the people in attendance at the rally. All classes are represented: "shopkeepers, artisans, pensioners, bureaucrats, students, white collar workers, many women and girls, but above all, numberless workers." "Troops of brown-shirts" also populate the hall, providing security for the assembly. These storm troopers, determined countenances upon their faces, are mostly workers, like Sturm. "God knows, these men do not look like bandits!"[8]

In stark contrast to the SA men is the band of "Communists and Red Front people" that sits in the middle of the crowd. A "Jewish-looking man," their leader, is making an anti-Nazi speech to his comrades and giving them schnapps. After several drinks, one of the Communists brags that "today we put an end to the Hitler trash!" Others yell "fascist dogs!" and "beat them all up!"[9]

The leader of the assembly tries to call the meeting to

order. The crowd begins to chant for order, and it appears that the meeting will degenerate into chaos. "The assembly leader stands as if carved from stone" and informs those present that they are in a "National Socialist Assembly" and that order will be maintained. His "determined words" cause the hall to grow silent. The "opponents" of the Nazis "feel that the assembly is in strong hands." The evening can proceed as planned.[10]

The speaker approaches the podium. He is a small man; one could mistake him for a "youth." But "every movement and every word" makes it clear that Joseph Goebbels is "a man." The title of the speech is "Lenin or Hitler." The Communists present, not liking the theme of the presentation, begin to interrupt the speaker. Goebbels deals with them forcefully, and they soon relent. "After five minutes all are dead quiet."[11]

Sturm has attended many political rallies. Berlin was, after all, the political center of Germany. But he has never seen anything comparable to this. Whereas the other assemblies were devoid of meaning, "here is determination and truth and here is the way!" Goebbels's speech was, in stark contrast to others he had heard, "powerfully clear." He is a man of action who will do what is necessary to redeem Germany. The speaker weeps as he recounts the shame his country has endured since the revolution. For the first time in his life, Sturm sees what the word *Volk* really means: every German is his "brother or sister." The speech exposes "a new world" to the mechanic.[12]

After Goebbels finishes, the discussion period begins. One of the Communists starts to spout the usual party line, making use of the standard terminology: "class-conscious proletariat" and "beat the fascists where you find them." Chaos results. The Communists begin to sing the "Internationale." In response, the leader of the SA guard blows his whistle. The situation deteriorates, and it soon becomes clear that a brawl is about to begin. Trying to preempt this possibility, the assembly leader shouts: "If you wish to settle the ideological struggle with chair legs and steel rods, we will counter your terror with even more brutal methods. Every attempt to break up the assembly will be beaten to the ground where it will suffocate in your blood."[13]

Sturm is impressed. Here are men who do not back down in the face of the enemy. They are willing to stand behind their ideas with their "blood and lives. . . . Here a new front presents itself, a resistance that is stronger than lies or gold." The fight begins. The Communists, singing the "Marseillaise," throw beer glasses and chair legs. "Tear down the flags!" someone with a knife in his hand cries. Because the Marxists have no respect for women, those present have to hide under tables to escape the indiscriminate Communist onslaught.[14]

The SA suddenly mounts a counterattack, the brave storm troopers assaulting the Communists in their rear and on their flanks. They beat the Marxist rabble "to the floor." The fight lasts only about two minutes. The enemy is forced to retreat with "bloody hands. . . . The fists of Germany's workers have really done their work!" The SA leader, "a gaping wound on his forehead," stands on a table, shouting, "Long live Germany!" The crowd responds with cheers and waving flags. "Three thousand arms are raised" in the Hitler salute. "Now Hans Sturm understands what the peculiar fascist salute represents: the noble consciousness of a great idea."[15]

This idea, for which "German workers . . . have fought and bled," will save Germany. Sturm realizes that "the time [is] at hand" for him to "give . . . [his] life to a heroic idea." So he "joins the National Socialist German Workers' Party," paying his membership fee with the money with that he had planned to spend celebrating the end of the work week. "'I thank you!' he says and shakes the speaker's hand. 'Now I know why I was put upon the earth.' And thus Hans Sturm finds the way to his *Volk* and becomes a soldier for the Third Reich."[16]

One can see several themes designed to appeal to the proletariat running throughout this story. The first of these, undoubtedly adopted from the propaganda techniques of the KPD, was the claim that the working man was unappreciated in the Weimar Republic. Sturm worked hard all week but had nothing to show for it. He had no family, no security, no one who cared about him. All the mechanic had to do on a Friday night was visit one of Berlin's numerous taverns or houses of ill repute. He was a lonely man living in a dismal city. "Hans Sturm's Awakening" implies that only the NSDAP really cared about people like Sturm. The Nazi *Weltanschauung* would provide meaning in his life.

Another major goal of this proletarian novel was to discredit "Marxist" claims concerning the composition and goals of the NSDAP. His fellow workers, undoubtedly duped by Communist propaganda, had told Sturm that Nazis were "bandits" and "killers of workers." In sharp contrast to the KPD line, those present, although representative of all classes, were primarily from the proletariat. Further driving this point home was Sturm's conclusion that the SA men at the assembly were brave, impressive looking, soldiers of the *Weltanschauung* of the future. "These men did not look like bandits!" Sturm concluded.

The Communists present, however, had little in common with the imposing figures the storm troopers presented. They were at the meeting, not to contribute anything positive to the evening's events but merely to cause trouble. As always, *Der Angriff* depicted Communist leaders as Jews. This was obvious from their appearance. One could always recognize these "bacilli" within the *Volksgemeinschaft*. Claims that Jews dominated the working-class parties were a consistent theme of Nazi appeals to workers.

The way the story recounted events during the assembly also maximized the novella's appeal to the proletariat. The Nazis, especially the leaders present, behaved in an orderly and, at times, heroic fashion. The assembly leader stood in the face of the Communist hecklers "as if carved in stone." The speaker, although slight in stature, was equally impressive, the logic of his arguments silencing even his most determined critics.

The fight that ensued at the end of the speech also presented the NSDAP in a positive light. It is important to note that it was the Communists who had started the brawl because they could not discredit Nazi ideology through peaceful argumentation. It was the Communists, not the SA men, who were the "bandits" and "murderers of workers." The storm troopers fought only in self defense, and they were willing to sacrifice their blood to defend their ideas. In addition, they fought in an orderly fashion, which was to be seen as indicative of working together for a common purpose.

All of these facts convinced Sturm that the NSDAP was the political movement that really had the benefit of the workers in mind. Therefore, he joined the NSDAP, becoming a "fighter" for the cause that would save not just the proletariat but all of Germany. The editors of *Der Angriff* hoped the readers of "Hans Sturms Erwachen" would arrive at the same conclusion.

"Hans Sturm's Awakening" also makes clear some other aspects of Nazi propaganda. First, it was almost totally negative in character. *Der Angriff* made no effort to present constructive criticism of the Weimar government. It did not try to present alternatives to the government's policies. The paper simply attacked everything connected with the *status quo*. In addition, Sturm's story illustrates the Nazi contention that all one had to do was accept the National Socialist *Weltanschauung* and his life would be changed completely. All troubles would end. This was an important component of Goebbels's propaganda technique: the NSDAP would solve all of Germany's problems if only given the chance.

These same themes, as well as many others, can be found in the other types of copy printed in the pages of *Der Angriff*. Hans Schweitzer, for example, drew many of his cartoons with an appeal to Berlin's workers in mind. They always depicted workers in a positive light, emphasizing the benefits that the proletariat would receive from the coming Third Reich. Political cartoons aimed at the proletariat fell into two large categories: those showing the advantages workers would have in the approaching National Socialist state (positive propaganda) and those attacking the working-class parties (negative propaganda). Among those fitting into the former category was one that appeared in the 14 May 1928 edition of *Der Angriff*. It

"Comrade! For a better future."

showed a storm trooper and a worker, hands joined, standing against a swastika in the background. The caption read, "Comrade! for a better future," the clear implication being that the NSDAP had the interests of the workers as its major goal. To further this impression, Schweitzer gave the SA man and the worker similar appearances. Both were stern and muscular, possessing serious countenances. It is clear from the drawing that the storm trooper is a worker, knows what would be best for the proletariat and is determined to pursue it.[17]

A drawing published in July 1928 graphically relates another popular propaganda motif of the Nazis: the end of class conflict. The cartoon shows two men, the one on the left obviously a white-collar worker and the other a laborer, the omnipresent hammer in his left hand. The white-collar worker is pointing toward the sun, clearly in reference to a brighter future. The two men have joined hands. In the background are symbols of the traditional social groups of Germany: a farm, a church, and a factory. The caption for the drawing reads: "Without free workers,—no free nation!" The clear implication was that, if all classes were willing to work together under the banner of National Socialism, Germany would see a better future.[18]

In sharp contrast to the way Schweitzer depicted the Nazi Party was the way he characterized the SPD and KPD. The Socialists and Communists, through their promotion of class antagonism, were the real "murderers of workers." RFB and Reichsbanner men left their proletarian victims lying in pools of blood in the gutter. This was all done at the behest of the Jews, who dominated these parties. A few examples will help establish this point.

In August 1928, *Der Angriff* published a cartoon that showed three RFB men dashing down the street. Wielding knives, they are fleeing two policemen approaching a body lying in the gutter. A short description to the left of the cartoon makes it clear that the victim is a member of the Stahlhelm, a right-wing paramilitary group that often allied itself with the Nazis. The caption underneath the cartoon says: "And it calls itself a Workers' Party!" The implication is, as always, quite clear. The three Communists, outnumbering their hapless victim, have seized an opportunity to do him in. The Communists are, as always, characterized as cowards, willing to fight only when they have a numerical advantage or a route of escape. Further, it is they who are killing Berlin's proletariat, not the NSDAP. Clearly, the cartoonist hoped to relate, the KPD did not deserve the epithet "Workers' Party."[19]

That all this was ultimately the work of the Jews, who dominated the working-class parties, was intimated in numerous cartoons. Among these is one that appeared in July 1928. This cartoon shows two men, obvious caricatures of Jews, pointing accusing fingers at each other. The man on the

"And it calls itself a workers' party."

"The thinking worker comes to Hitler."

left is identified as a Communist by the masthead of *Rote Fahne* appearing behind him. The masthead of *Vorwaerts* appearing in the background clearly identifies the man on the right as a Socialist. The two are screaming insults at each other, each accusing the other of being a "traitor to the workers [*Arbeiterverraeter*]!!!" Between the two men stands a worker clearly indifferent to them. The caption reads: "The THINKING Worker comes to HITLER." The inference here is that the two "proletarian" parties were too busy fighting each other to pursue the benefit of the workers, and if a worker took the time to think about it, he would come to this realization as well and turn to the NSDAP, the only truly working-class party.[20]

A similar cartoon, appearing in November 1929 shows workers coming over to the Nazis from the KPD. A Jew, trying to impede the progress of the converts, is blocking their way, shouting, "Beat the fascists where you encounter them!" On his arm is printed "red lies." But the Jew cannot stop all of the workers who wish to join the NSDAP, and some manage to get through to the waiting Nazi. The man welcoming the workers to the Nazi movement is also a laborer as is shown by the hammer hanging from his belt. The caption above reads: "Red murder-slogan—last hopeless means of maintaining members." "The upright workers open their eyes" is printed below. This cartoon is representative of Nazi claims that the only thing standing between the proletariat and the liberation of the toiling classes was the "Jewish dominated" parties, and realizing this was the first step in solving the problem.[21]

Many of the articles in *Der Angriff* also castigated the proletarian parties. The headline of the 14 May 1928 edition, for example, read: "Marxist Treason Time and Time Again." The accompanying article was an acidic critique of the SPD's acceptance of the Dawes Plan, under which Germany agreed upon a schedule of payments for the reparations incurred as a result of its role in the First World War. The plan, *Der Angriff* insisted, made Germany a "colony" of "high-finance." It was the German Socialist Party that had agreed to these dishonorable demands. Indeed, it was representatives of the SPD who had signed the "Versailles Peace-Diktat." By doing so "the German Social Democratic Party has accepted the guilt for the war in principle; the Social Democratic Party should be ashamed to have made such a declaration." Because of its acceptance of the War-Guilt Lie and the rest of the Treaty of Versailles, the SPD had left the German people in a condition of "destitution and need." Such conduct made it clear that the SPD was not the party of Germany's proletariat—which suffered because of reparations—but of British and French capitalists, who were the true beneficiaries of its policies.[22]

An article appearing in July 1928 strove to drive home a similar point. The story revolves around the scholarly activities of a captain on the general staff, A. Heider. Heider, through the use of previously untapped sources, determined that the French commander, General Joffre, had planned to violate Switzerland's neutrality in the opening days of the war, hoping to outflank the Germans. Joffre, however, stopped the troops just short of the border. Germany's invasion of neutral Belgium, on the other hand, was a response to this French plan, and hence, by the terms of the logic employed in *Der Angriff*, France's responsibility. The Marxist and bourgeois papers, the Nazi organ pointed out, had not picked up this story. This was further evidence that Germany's Marxists and democrats had abandoned the nation's proletariat. After all, it was Germany's working people who had to pay the price incurred because of the "War-Guilt Lie."[23]

The editors of *Der Angriff* sought not only to discredit SPD and KPD claims to be working-class parties; they tried also to establish that the Nazi Party was concerned with the well-being of Germany's proletariat. A 16 April 1928 article, for example, chastised the Reichsbahn for laying off two thousand workers. *Der Angriff* explained these layoffs, as it did every other negative development during this period, as a product of the poor economic conditions resulting from the Dawes Plan. The piece continued by stating that the layoffs could have been avoided if the government had raised ticket prices and freight rates. It was unwilling to do so, however, because an election was approaching, and democratic governments were inherently more interested in winning elections and maintaining the backing of capitalists than they were in doing what was best for the people. Once again, Germany's government, dominated by the SPD, had sold out the workers at the behest of high finance. The article implied that this would not be the case under a National Socialist government.[24]

Another article published in 1928 dealt with working conditions among post office employees. *Der Angriff* claimed that the board of directors of the post office had unilaterally increased hours of operation without consulting postal workers. The board did this, the paper pointed out, in a so-called "workers' democracy." In addition, the routes of letter carriers remained unchanged since the war, in spite of the fact that there were now many more addresses to which mail had to be delivered. To make matters worse, in order to increase operating hours, service had to be cut back and workers had to put in more hours without an appropriate increase in compensation. Postal workers also had to buy new uniforms, which the paper saw as an unnecessary financial burden. This would serve to benefit the firms that sold postal uniforms, many of which were owned by Jews. The article concluded with a call to the board of directors to rescind these measures for the benefit of the workers in order to avoid a "breakdown of the abandoned postal carriers." This article is significant because it shows that the editors of *Der Angriff* were, on occasion, willing to attack specific problems and offer detailed solutions which would benefit Germany's proletariat. For the most part, however, the paper was unwilling to make any concrete proposals and concentrated its efforts upon negative propaganda designed to discredit the Weimar Republic.[25]

Appeals to the proletariat continued throughout the "years of struggle" as is evinced by the lead story of a special election edition appearing in November 1932. The headline read: "Against Hugenberg-Capitalism; Against Pride of Place and Class Hate." The accompanying story denied charges made in the publications of the ultraconservative Scherl-Verlag that

Der Angriff was not a *voelkisch* publication. In response, Goebbels's daily charged that not only was the local Scherl-Verlag publication, the *Berliner Lokal-Anzeiger*, run by Jews but it was not interested in the benefit of the *Volk* at all. The Nazis, on the other hand, were, according to *Der Angriff*, interested in improving the lives of the German people. After all, the Berlin Nazi organ had continually opposed Germany's "policy of compliance" with the Treaty of Versailles. Because of the government's policies, the NSDAP had chosen to oppose the hated system at every turn. For this reason, the Nazi party had grown to a strength of 14 million and was on the verge of victory.[26]

In response to these actions, the conservative press had written that: "Goebbels is the masculine Rosa Luxemburg. Both are undistinguished in form and Jewish in appearance. He sets in motion—as she did earlier—a great burning passion to hate and to lie." That the Scherl-Verlag was willing to make such outrageous statements was presented as evidence that it was the conservative press that lied. Indeed, the Scherl-Verlag was without honor. It was, after all, the tool of "high finance" and others who supported submission in the face of the Versailles Treaty. The policies of Hugenberg and the conservatives had driven the proletariat into the arms of the Marxist parties. In contrast, Goebbels and the Berlin NSDAP had "made red Berlin German again," because they were willing to pursue policies that benefited the workers, not the capitalists. As usual the nature of the Nazi Party's proletarian program was not explicitly spelled out. In general, *Der Angriff* chose to concentrate upon negative propaganda, attacking its enemies without offering any concrete alternatives.[27]

The most important occasion upon which *Der Angriff* took the side of Berlin's working class was during the Berlin Transportation (BVG) strike of November 1932. Although the strike lasted only a few days, the violent clashes between the police and strikers probably had an effect upon subsequent parliamentary elections, hurting those parties which supported the republic. The immediate catalyst for the outbreak of the strike was a salary reduction of two pfennigs per hour imposed upon BVG employees, but there were political motivations for the work stoppage that went well beyond a pay dispute.[28]

The BVG strike was part of a larger KPD strategy to discredit the Socialist trade unions (German Trade Union Federation, or ADGB) among Germany's workers and win the proletariat over to the KPD's Revolutionary Trade Union Opposition (RGO). The Communist Party hoped to accomplish this by fomenting worker unrest wherever possible. They hoped this would lead to a strike that the ADGB would refuse to support. When the KPD, in contrast to the Socialists, stood behind the work stoppage, it could thereafter claim to be the only legitimate voice of Germany's working classes. In short, the primary motivation of the KPD leadership to strike was political, not material. From May to October 1932, the RGO led over eight hundred strikes throughout Germany.[29]

From the point of view of the Communists, the BVG was an attractive target politically. Located in the German capital, it was highly visible. Further, it was the third-largest corporation in Germany, employing over 23,000 workers. It was publicly owned, making it probable that the Socialist trade unions would not support a strike. Finally, the forced pay decrease came at a fortuitous time politically for the KPD, just before the 6 November 1932 elections. Discrediting the SPD could very well win proletarian votes for the Communists in the approaching contest. Also, a work stoppage aimed at such an important target could lead to a general strike, paving the way to revolution.[30]

The strike vote took place on 2 November 1932. Of the 23,000 people employed by the BVG, 18,500 voted. Seventy-eight percent (about 14,040) voted to stop work. In spite of the fact that a large majority favored walking out, the SPD refused to sanction the strike. It insisted that a strike could only be called when a three-quarters majority of all BVG workers voted in favor of a walkout. Therefore, the Socialists claimed, a strike was only justified when 17,250 BVG employees voted in favor of a work stoppage. This refusal to support the action of the Berlin transport workers would cost the SPD dearly in the approaching election.[31]

When twenty thousand of Berlin's transport workers went

on strike on the morning of 3 November, Goebbels and the Berlin NSDAP found themselves in a difficult situation. The Nazi trade union, the National Socialist Organization of Shop Stewards (NSBO), had made significant inroads into the BVG. To refuse to support the strike could destroy the work done with the transportation workers as well as other proletarian supporters of the NSDAP. To stand behind the transport workers also presented hazards. For the NSDAP to ally itself with the KPD, a party that it insisted was a tool of the "international world Jewish conspiracy," could cause it to lose the support of many of its conservative backers. To Goebbels, however, it was clear that the Nazis had to support a strike, the goal of which was to secure the "most primitive rights of life [Lebensrechte]" for a significant portion of Berlin's proletariat. Also, this action would help debunk claims that the NSDAP was just another "bourgeois" party unconcerned with the welfare of the people. On the other hand, Goebbels was sensitive to claims that the walkout was part of a "Bolshevik" plot. In the end, however, he was able to convince Hitler that supporting the transport workers was the lesser of two evils. Indeed, such a course could gain support for the NSDAP in the approaching election. This hope, however, would prove futile.[32]

On the morning of 3 November 1932, Berliners awoke to a city without subway or train services. Although strikebreakers were willing to operate some of the street cars, this means of transportation proved hazardous since strikers threw large stones at the cars as they drove past. At first, about 3,600 transport employees were willing to work. This violent campaign against strikebreakers proved effective, however, and by 5 November only 1,900 BVG workers showed up at their jobs.[33]

The three major political parties in Berlin each took a different line on the strike. The SPD contended that the Communists—whom it referred to as "Kozis"—were the mere lackeys of the Nazis. *Vorwaerts* insisted that the BVG strike was but a prelude to a putsch. The Nazis and the "Kozis," it held, were trying to overthrow violently the democratically elected government of Germany. *Rote Fahne* received a nine-day prohibition on 4 November, limiting the KPD's capability of presenting its account of the strike. An article appearing on 3 November, however, made it clear that the Communist Party was unwilling to give its temporary ally, the NSDAP, any credit for the progress of the strike. Members of the NSBO, the article suggested, were trying to break the strike. The Nazis had opposed the walkout, and the meager support they now gave was nothing more than unadulterated opportunism. Indeed, in the past, Goebbels and the Nazis had opposed most strikes and would not have supported this one if they were not concerned with maintaining the votes of their working-class supporters in the upcoming election. Another article on the same page related the Communist view of the SPD's role in the strike. The Socialists had, *Rote Fahne* maintained, betrayed the proletariat and worked out a deal with Chancellor Papen under which they would form a coalition with Papen and the Nazis. The SPD's primary goal was, as always, political power, not the benefit of the workers.[34]

The Nazis, like the Communists, chastised the SPD for its attitude during the strike. In an article appearing on the first day of the walkout, *Der Angriff* insisted that the strike was necessary in the face of the Socialist Party's policies toward Germany's workers. After all, the SPD's "politics of corruption" were responsible for the current economic plight, which had caused the BVG to demand a reduction in pay from its employees. It was unconscionable, the paper insisted, to ask transport workers to take a pay cut at the same time that the BVG was increasing fares. In the eyes of *Der Angriff*, this was just further proof that the system created by the Social Democrats was corrupt and that, in spite of its protestations to the contrary, the SPD did not care about the proletariat. In short, the "reduction in wages" and the resulting strike were "the result" of "years of Social Democratic mismanagement of the economy."[35]

Violent clashes between strikers and the police provided an atmosphere in which a journal like *Der Angriff* flourished. The death of a forty-six-year-old storm trooper and customs employee, Kurt Reppich, in a clash with police on Martin-Luther-Strasse in Schoeneberg provided the paper with an opportunity to incorporate the "death myth" into pro-strike propaganda. During the very early hours of 4 November, Reppich's *Sturm* 13, as well as numerous other SA *Sturme* and SS men, were demonstrating on Wartzburgplatz in favor of the strike. At around 5:00 A.M. the police tried to break up the assembly. A violent confrontation soon developed in which the police made liberal use of their billy clubs. During the course of the brawl, Reppich was shot in the head. He died in St. Norbert's Hospital. Another storm trooper was shot in the upper arm.[36]

Der Angriff grasped the opportunity to proclaim Reppich a martyr for the workers' cause. Reppich had gathered with other National Socialists—workers, white-collar employees, transportation employees, and bureaucrats—in order to demonstrate his "solidarity with the BVG employees struggling against the oppressive pay reduction." He, like all the other Nazis, was "standing peacefully on the street." The police burst upon the scene suddenly, attacking the protestors without provocation. In spite of the fact that the demonstrators had no weapons, the police made use of their pistols against the defenseless crowd. The wounded "lay in their blood." It was clear, in the opinion of *Der Angriff*, that the "police had . . . no grounds for shooting." In response to the actions of the officers the people of the neighborhood took to the streets, demanding justice and an end to the "murder" of innocent workers. Like all other Nazi martyrs, the death of Reppich was a call to action for anyone concerned with Germany's welfare.[37]

Another article explained the cause for which Reppich had given his life: the benefit of Berlin's working classes. Brave men, like Reppich, who were willing to stand up for what they knew was right, had shut down the BVG. Early on the morning of 3 November 1932, transport workers, accompanied by "workers, shop owners, white-collar workers, students and the unemployed," had marched upon train stations, where the police confronted them. The workers were: "not thinking of storming, of attacking, of blasting or of destroying. They demand their rightful pay and will not permit themselves to be oppressed into a condition of slave labor."[38]

The deeds of the strikers and their supporters were, according to *Der Angriff*, an excellent example of the *Volksgemein-schaft* in action. People of all classes had worked together in order to benefit the German people. The BVG strike was not the product of class consciousness but of *voelkisch* consciousness. The German people should work together, not against each other. The strikers wanted to help create a "new state of na-tional honor and social justice." "This is our [National Social-ism's] final goal." The protests were unbelligerent, but the po-lice employed by the system had broken the peace and beaten and shot SA men in the streets. The people had not tolerated this, and they had taken action. Further, Reppich's comrades, after dipping a Nazi flag in the dead storm trooper's blood, had carried it through the neighborhoods of Berlin, returning it to his *Sturm's* tavern. They were showing their appreciation for a fallen comrade, former front-line soldier, leader and fa-ther. Reppich, the article makes clear, was but one of many "disciplined" storm troopers who had peacefully stood up to the police, only to have their lives taken from them. The death of this ordinary, yet heroic, man would inspire others to follow in his steps. National Socialism, therefore, could not be de-feated. In the end, men such as Reppich, who were willing to die for the *Volksgemeinschaft*, would emerge victorious.[39]

Although *Der Angriff*, as was typical of its approach to pro-paganda, emphasized the violent aspects of the BVG strike, the paper addressed other issues as well. One of the major prob-lems the strike caused for the Nazis stemmed from the fact that they had allied themselves with the Communist Party, Nazism's sworn enemy. On 5 November 1932, *Der Angriff* pub-lished a speech given by Goebbels in which the Gauleiter dealt with this seeming inconsistency. The Nazis simply could not help it, Goebbels contended, if the KPD "thinks like us for once." This strike, the speaker claimed, had nothing to do with "class struggle" and everything to do with class cooperation. People of all strata supported the strike because it was just. National Socialism, as the vanguard of the new Germany, was obligated to endorse any strike that benefited the Reich. The BVG walkout clearly fell into this category. An article appear-ing the previous day, "The NSDAP supports every justified strike," took the same line. It insisted that, contrary to what the Communist press held, it was not unusual for the Nazis to support a work stoppage. The article even gave a list of sixteen strikes the NSDAP had supported in 1931 alone.[40]

Neither the Nazis nor the transport workers, however, were the primary beneficiaries of the strike. The KPD was. Reichstag elections took place in the midst of the conflagration. The Communist Party received 860,000 votes in Berlin, making it the largest political faction in the capital. The Nazis, losing around 36,000 votes in Berlin, suffered a major setback throughout Germany. The SPD lost over 75,000 votes in the German capital. The transport workers emerged from the conflict having done no better. Eleven thousand members of the Communist trade unions, having accomplished their primary goal, winning worker support away from the Socialists, returned to work on election day. Support for the strike quickly faded. The KPD, which had been the primary mover behind the 2-3 November walkout, had, in effect, also broken the strike.[41]

There are several conclusions that can be drawn concerning *Der Angrif's* appeals to the proletariat. These conclusions affect at least three important historiographic arguments. The first of these is concerned with the contention that, after the debacle of the May 1928 Reichstag elections, Nazi propaganda shifted away from a concentration upon the proletariat and toward an appeal to the peasantry. Many within the Nazi leadership thought this was the case, Otto Strasser being only the most obvious example.

Evidence culled from *Der Angriff*, however, indicates that the situation was much more complicated than most historians have claimed. It is clear that *Der Angriff* aimed its appeal primarily at Berlin's workers throughout the "years of struggle." There was no dramatic change in its propaganda line after May 1928. This was the case primarily because Berlin had a large proletarian population. Goebbels and his staff simply had no choice but to continue their appeal to the working classes. It can safely be concluded, therefore, that, while the national leadership may have changed its propaganda strategy, local leaders had a great deal of latitude in determining propaganda tactics at the Gau level. This was clearly the case when it came to the motifs employed by Goebbels and *Der Angriff.*[42]

This claim affects another major dispute among historians: that concerning the character of Nazi intra-party politics. Was Hitler in complete control of the party, or was the NSDAP a chaotic organization, consisting of numerous factions, each trying to pursue its own agenda? The fact that Goebbels, and by extension probably other regional Nazi leaders, could adapt his propaganda to local conditions leads one to conclude that the NSDAP was not completely unified ideologically. Other Nazi newspapers, Julius Streicher's *Der Stuermer* for example, pursued a somewhat different propaganda strategy from *Der Angriff.* Whereas the Berlin paper concentrated its efforts upon appeals to the proletariat, *Der Stuermer's* infamous pornographic anti-Semitism attracted the uneducated rural population. This leads one to conclude that those who view the Nazi Party as a "polycratic" organization—one representing numerous groups with varying interests, each having a share of power within the party and later the Third Reich—are nearer the truth than the "Hitler centrists."[43]

Yet another major historiographic dispute concerns the alleged "antimodern" nature of National Socialism. Historians Michael Burleigh and Wolfgang Wippermann have called this issue "among the most crucial problems confronting modern historical research." On the surface, the fact that *Der Angriff* concentrated its appeals upon Berlin's workers discredits claims made by George Mosse and others that National Socialism was primarily an antimodern phenomenon. On the other hand, the techniques employed by the paper to appeal to workers were clearly antimodernist. The Nazis, unlike unquestionably modern parties such as the SPD and the KPD, did not try to appeal to the workers as a class. *Der Angriff* continually attacked such ideas as "class consciousness" and "class conflict." The Berlin NSDAP approached the proletariat as an "estate." The working class was an integral part of society and, as such, was obligated to work together with other Germans for the benefit of the entire nation. The proletariat's primary concern was to be the interests of the

Volk, not of the workers. In short, *Der Angriff's* propaganda tried to help create the *Volksgemeinschaft* (people's community), which played such an important role in Nazi ideology. Class conflict was counterproductive to achieving this goal. The paper therefore did all it could to discredit the Communist Party's attempts to promote class hatred.[44]

The goal of creating a *Volksgemeinschaft* was clearly a rejection of the Enlightenment's call for racial and religious tolerance. It was a throwback to nineteenth-century romanticism, to a mythical view of the Middle Ages. This new community the Nazis hoped to create would consist of all people of German blood working together for a common goal, the improvement of Germany. There would be no exploitation of the workers as was the case under capitalism, and the class conflict that Marxist ideology fostered would also be absent. All Germans would live together peacefully. In short, the Nazis hoped to create a nationalist and racist utopia. The propaganda presented in *Der Angriff* was a first tentative step in creating the conditions under which this paradise could be created.

Other aspects of *Der Angriff's* appeal to the workers were clearly antimodern in nature. The anti-Semitism that permeated the paper's copy was also the product of a premodern bias. As Burleigh and Wippermann have argued, nineteenth- and twentieth-centry anti-Semitism were, to a large extent, reactions against industrialzation and the alienation it produced, especially among the middle classes. Since Jewish emancipation occurred within the same time frame as industrialzation and the growth of capitalism, the Jews were often linked with these developments, especially with their negative aspects. Further, the emphasis upon heroic death in *Der Angriff* was also the result of a premodern world view. Therefore, it is clear that, while appeals to the proletariat were clearly a realistic concession to the twentieth century, the ways in which *Der Angriff* attempted to attract working-class support were the products of an antimodern *Weltanschauung*.[45]

6

The "System"

According to *Der Angriff*, the Weimar system was responsible for all of Germany's ills. Because of the "un-German" democracy created by the Social Democrats—who had stabbed the gallant German Army in the back during the closing days of the war—the nation had suffered the humiliation of the Versailles "Diktat" and the resulting collapse of the its economy.

Because it was created by "traitors" who had abandoned the brave men dying at the front in favor of a "Marxist" revolution, *Der Angriff* held that the republic was illegitimate from its inception. Not only had the "November Criminals" turned their backs on Germany in the closing days of the war, but they had also signed the hated Versailles Treaty, which had enslaved Germany to the erstwhile Entente powers. To make matters worse, the republic had compounded its sin by agreeing to the hated Dawes and Young Plans, under which the Weimar government recognized the legitimacy of reparations. Because the traitors had made these agreements, the German economy was in a state of chaos, and unemployment was widespread. The actions of the November Criminals, the founders of the hated republic, were the cause of all this suffering.[1]

Indeed, self-interest was, in the eyes of Goebbels's paper, the most conspicuous characteristic of Weimar Germany's leadership. According to *Der Angriff*, corruption was rampant within the system. In an article entitled "Parliamentarianism is Corruption," *Der Angriff* bemoaned the fact that the Reichstag had increased its expense allowances at a time when many Germans were unemployed and in need. The paper cited this as a typical example of the callous disregard the Reichstag exhibited when it was to the advantage of its members. In yet another piece, the paper interpreted the government's "shameless" tax policies as further evidence that the system sought its own advantage to the detriment of the *Volk*. Taxes on working and farming families were raised in order to pay the fourteen billion marks per year in reparations incurred because of the Dawes Plan. While the burden upon the common people increased, the leaders of the "Daweskolonie" had decreased taxes upon the wealthy. This was further evidence that the system considered the leaders of finance capital the most important people in Germany. After all, only the wealthy could provide the monetary backing that was the lifeblood of Germany's political parties. Further, many Reichstag members, being wealthy themselves, benefited from these policies. In short, the system was concerned only with its own interests and cared little about the common people.[2]

Der Angriff had a simple explanation for the corruption of the system. Jews dominated it. The logic employed by Goebbels and his underlings was simple. The Jews dominated the "Marxist" parties, and the SPD dominated the system. Therefore, the Jews controlled the system that enslaved Germany. Ultimately the Jews were responsible for all of Germany's ills. Not only did the paper's copy make this contention clear but so did its political cartoons. Schweitzer always portrayed the leaders of the Weimar Republic as Jewish caricatures. This alleged connection between the Jews and the system was the subject of some of *Der Angriff's* most virulent anti-Semitic propaganda.[3]

Bernhard Weiss, the vice president of the Berlin Police Force, and also a Jew and member of the Democratic Party, provided a particularly attractive target for *Der Angriff's* attacks upon the system. Weiss, who was trained as a lawyer and soon became a judge, earned an Iron Cross First Class during the war. Following the war, he joined the Berlin Police

Force, his talent enabling him quickly to rise to the leadership of the criminal police. Weiss became the number two man in the police department in 1927, shortly after Goebbels became Gauleiter. Soon Weiss was known in right-wing circles by the abusive name "Isidor." Use of Weiss's nickname became so widespread that many people were unaware that it was not his real name. Goebbels and the staff of *Der Angriff* played a vital role in bringing this about. An ongoing battle between Weiss and Goebbels, fought in the courts and on the pages of the Gau's newspaper, characterized Berlin politics for the next three years.[4]

An article published in *Der Angriff* in October 1927 explained why the Nazis had chosen the apellation Isidor for Weiss. The custom of dubbing one's enemies with derisive names based upon their physiognomy was, according to the author of the piece, a tradition that went back to the Roman Empire (*"Nomen est omen"*). It was only natural, therefore, that Weiss be called Isidor. The Greek word *dor* meant gift, and *Isi* was short for the goddess Isis. Isidor meant "gift of Isis." Isis was a major Egyptian deity; hence Isidor also meant "gift of Egypt." Egypt was, according to *Der Angriff*, the source of much of the world's evil: the gypsies and "above all the Jews." The Bible also held that the Jews had come out of Egypt. Since Weiss was a Jew, this transparent pseudointellectual argument concluded, it was only natural that he be dubbed Isidor, "gift from Egypt." The name, according to the newspaper, was not so much an insult as an accurate description of who Weiss was. This argument would often surface as a defense in libel suits brought by the police vice president against *Der Angriff*.[5]

Although the conflict between Weiss and Goebbels began with Nazi placards and speeches, it intensified after the police banned the party in May 1927. The 8-9 May 1927 issue of the *Voelkischer Beobachter* published a vicious polemic aimed at discrediting the police vice president. The lead story, "Violations of the Constitution by the Jewish-Marxist Berlin Police," charged that the prohibition issued against the Berlin NSDAP was a violation of the right to free speech guaranteed

Es ist schlechthin erschütternd.

Nun haben wir uns ein ganzes Jahr hindurch soviel Mühe gegeben, dies edle Antlitz populär zu machen, und jetzt müssen wir es erleben, daß alle unsere Bemühungen sich als erfolglos erwiesen.

Nicht einmal seine eigene Garde weiß, wie ihr oberster Kriegsherr aussieht. „Was, Du Affe!" sagt so ein grüner Grenadier und beweist damit seine mangelnde zoologische Kenntnis; denn statt einer platten Affennase verfügt im vorliegenden Falle das also angeredete Wesen über einen unbedingt wuchtig ausgebildeten Gesichtserker.

Man möchte sagen: mehr Erker als Gesicht. Platt sind da ganz andere Extremitäten.

Aber als echte Nationalsozialisten verlieren wir den Mut nicht und bringen noch einmal das mit der ganzen Liebe unseres Herzens gezeichnete Conterfei des Polizeivizepräsidenten

Dr. Bernhard Weiß,

Sohn des Großkaufmanns Max Weiß, Parforcereiter, Kurator der „Hochschule für die Wissenschaft des Judentums." Die „Jüdischliberale Zeitung"

vom 8. Juni 1928 schreibt über ihn unter der Ueberschrift: „Jüdische Köpfe" voll Begeisterung: „Wir preisen die Unerschrockenheit, Zähigkeit und Ausdauer von Bernhard Weiß und wünschen ihm und uns Glück zu seinen Wegen und Zielen."

Nun, wenn das jüdische Volk sich Glück wünscht zu den Wegen und Zielen von Bernhard Weiß, dann kann das deutsche Volk sich wohl auch gratulieren.

Oder nicht?

"This is what he [Bernhard Weiss] looks like!"

by the Weimar constitution. A large picture of Weiss appeared under the headline. Above the picture was the caption "This is what he looks like! [*So sieht er aus!*]," the Nazis contending that Weiss's appearance made it evident that he was Jewish. The police vice president refused to take this insult lying down and took Goebbels to court for defamation of character, thus beginning a series of legal battles between Weiss and the NSDAP that would continue over the next three years.[6]

Wer wählt Liste „Sechs" (Demokraten)?

Nur der Gerr mit den entsprechenden Nasen!

"Who votes list 'six' (Democrats)? Only people with the appropriate noses."

Weiss's "Jewish" countenance remained a major theme in the political cartoons in *Der Angriff*. Drawings of Weiss always contained the prominent hooked nose that was so prevalent in anti-Semitic caricatures. A cartoon appearing during the May 1928 Reichstag election, for example, showed the police vice president standing in line, waiting to cast his vote. On his ballot appears the numeral six, the number of the list of the Democrats. Weiss's nose is also shown as containing the outline of a six. The clear implication of this cartoon was that those who voted for the Democrats were also supporting Weiss and the rest of the Jews who dominated the system. Another caricature depicted Weiss's face on a donkey, implying that he was an ass (*Esel*).[7]

Isidor, as a tool of the system, was allegedly a callous individual who did not care about the welfare of the German people. The actions of the Berlin police after the 1927 party

Bernhard Weiss as "The New Nero."

congress in Nuremberg served as proof that the police force, dominated by men like Weiss, was a brutal puppet of the system. When the Nazis returning from Nuremberg arrived at the train station, the Berlin police were there to greet them. They arrested some 500 Nazis for violating the prohibition on the NSDAP. As a result, they all missed a day of work, 74 of them losing their jobs. The actions of the police had, in the eyes of *Der Angriff*, "made 74 workers breadless." This was, in the end, a victory for the Nazis, since the "hunger pains should help" remind these workers who was responsible for their plight. A caricature of Weiss appearing in December 1927 dubbed him "The New Nero." The cartoon showed Weiss dressed in a toga, policemen standing behind him in the uniforms of Roman centurions. Standing before Weiss was an SA man tied to a post with the word *Verbot* upon it. The implication of this cartoon was clear. National Socialism was a new movement, persecuted by authorities who wanted to suppress the truth. In this it was much like first-century Christianity.[8]

A piece from September 1927 provides an excellent example of the paper's contention that the Berlin Police Department was a vicious, heartless organization. *Der Angriff* reported that, while on her way home from a Nazi meeting with her husband, a woman identified only as Mrs. Dornbusch was assaulted by the police after someone nearby shouted, *"Deutschland erwache!"* Not only was Mrs. Dornbusch beaten by the officers, she was also arrested. Things only got worse for the poor woman. A "fat . . . [police] commissar named Hoehne" decided that, since Frau Dornbusch was in jail, there was no one to take care of her six-year-old child. Hoehne wanted to take the child to the orphanage. Not only had the police forbidden Dornbusch from exercising her right to demonstrate for the NSDAP, but it also tried to "rob her child" from her. Clearly, the system had gone too far in this instance.[9]

On another occasion, *Der Angriff* claimed, the police had been warned two hours in advance about a planned Communist attack upon storm troopers in the Goerlitzer train station but had done nothing to prevent it. This was typical, the article went on to say, of the way that the system yielded in the face of the red terror. The RFB waged "open civil war" on the streets of Berlin, not only against the Nazis but also the people of Berlin and the policemen themselves. Yet the police were concerned primarily with crushing the Nazi Party, the only true representatives of the *Volk*.[10]

But such actions on the part of the police were, in the eyes of *Der Angriff*, typical. The police had, the paper contended, consistently assaulted people participating in peaceful demonstrations. One Nazi, the butcher Herbert Guenz, for example, was assaulted by five men (allegedly Jewish friends of the police) as the police looked on. When he began to fight back, the policemen responded by beating Guenz with their billy clubs. This was in sharp contrast to official policy, which stated that the police were obligated to protect those participating in a peaceful assembly. This hypocrisy, however, was indicative of the injustice inherent in the system. Another major theme of *Der Angriff*'s attacks upon the Berlin police was alleged corruption. A story appearing in December 1927 charged that the police held parties with official money. Also, the wife of the police president received the use of a horse at taxpayers' expense. The police force, like all other parts of the Weimar system, was ridden with corruption.[11]

Der Angriff often singled out Weiss as a specific target for similar attacks, particularly in political cartoons. These cartoons depicted Weiss as single-minded and ruthless in his persecution of Berlin's Nazis. A December 1927 cartoon, for example, was entitled "Isidor, if he would have celebrated Christmas." The cartoon shows Weiss, callous as ever, hanging dead SA men upon his Christmas tree. At the top of the tree is a Star of David. The gramophone is playing "Daughter of Zion be Joyful." At the right is a dog with a policeman's head, clearly implying that policemen are mere lackeys of Weiss, the persecutor of the NSDAP. Another cartoon showed Weiss astride a rocking horse, calling the dogs of the Socialist Party to the hunt. The intended victim of the chase was the NSDAP, represented by a majestic elk. The title of the cartoon was "The 'hunt' begins." Yet another caricature of Weiss depicted him as a boxer. Before him was a punching bag with the word *Constitution* upon it. The caption read: "The daily morning training of a well-known political knock-out artist." The implication of this cartoon was clear: Weiss's support for the Weimar constitution was not only one of convenience, it was also inconsistent. While standing steadfast behind it, the police vice president was more than willing to batter the constitution when it suited him.[12]

In general, *Der Angriff's* depiction of the Berlin Police Force was designed to enhance the image of the NSDAP as a persecuted movement. The Nazis were trying to overthrow the evil system, which was merely a tool the Jews used to keep Germany subjugated. In the face of the Nazis' unrelenting onslaught, the system had turned its police upon the peaceful Nazi Party. Weimar authorities could not keep the NSDAP under control by the nonviolent means consistent with the Weimar constitution. Like every other wing of the system, the Jews dominated the police force. Further, the police force was the backbone of the system, because without its violent

Tägliches Morgentraining

eines bekannten politischen Knock-out-Boxers

Bernhard Weiss batters the constitution.

actions against the German people, the *Volk* would rise up and overthrow the republic, thereby redeeming Germany. It was the fist of the system. Bernhard Weiss served as an excellent symbol for the system because he was a leader of the Berlin Police Force and was Jewish. Also, he fought the Nazis at every turn, determined not to let SA thugs have free rein in his city. While Weiss's actions helped to make the streets of Berlin safer, they also had the unfortunate result of feeding into *Der Angriff's* propaganda. Prohibitions and violent clashes between the Nazis and the police only served to enhance the image of the party among opponents of the Weimar Republic. Because the system hated by so many was determined to crush the NSDAP, the Nazis became heroes in the minds of many people. Thus a major goal of Goebbels's propaganda was attained.

The victims of *Der Angriff's* hyperbole, however, were not without recourse. From the outset, the paper faced numerous legal challenges in the form of libel suits. After the enactment of the changes in the Reich Press Law in 1930, bans upon *Der Angriff's* publication became a frequent alternative to libel actions.

During the first three years of the paper's publication, however, libel suits were the only option open to victims of *Der Angriff's* enmity who did not wish to let Goebbels's insults pass unopposed. Weiss, the public figure most often attacked on the pages of the paper, was among the most frequent plaintiffs in these cases. He accused *Der Angriff* of libel at least three times during the first six months of the paper's publication. These and subsequent suits brought against Goebbels and other leaders of the paper's editorial staff had mixed success. While Goebbels, Duerr, or Lippert often received fines and prison terms as a result of these suits, Goebbels used his immunity as a member of the Reichstag to avoid serving jail terms. Further, these attacks upon *Der Angriff* served as ammunition for the paper's propaganda against the system.[13]

One of the first cases Weiss brought against *Der Angriff* involved a series of articles published in the paper during the last three months of 1927, as well as two political cartoons. The articles appeared under the rubric, "Danger! Rubber Clubs." They were vicious personal attacks, chastising "Isidor" for cowardice, insisting that he was using the power of the Berlin Police Force to attack the fledgling NSDAP, thereby pursuing the goals of the Jewish-dominated system. "You should be ashamed of yourself, Isidor," the paper concluded. One of the offensive cartoons was the one depicting Weiss's face on the body of a donkey. The other related *Der Angriff's*

„Bernhard": „Verbieten? — Wiefo? — Hat er einen Juden angefaßt?"

"'Bernhard': 'Prohibited?—How come?—Has he attacked a Jew?'"

position on Weiss's recent prohibition of the Communist Red
Front Fighters' League. The cartoon showed an SA man talk-
ing to the police vice president and pointing at two RFB men.
The caption read: "'Bernhard:' 'Prohibited?—How come—
Has he assaulted a Jew?'" The implication was that Weiss
did not care for the storm troopers assaulted by the RFB, only
for his fellow Jews.[14]

The indictment in this case named Dagobert Duerr, the
author of the articles, as the primary defendant with Goebbels, publisher of the paper and Schulze, *Der Angriff's* printer,
named as co-defendants. While the court acquitted Schulze,
holding that he was not responsible for the newspaper's contents, it handed down guilty verdicts against Duerr and Goebbels. The court ruled that the use of the name Isidor to identify
Weiss was libel, because it presented Weiss in a "hateful, unworthy manner" and strove "to make him [appear] comical."
One of the articles also referred to Weiss as a "butcher of work-

ers [*Arbeiterschlaechter*], which contains a stark impression of misconduct." "They [the attacks] are therefore libelous." The court also judged the caricature of Weiss being addressed by the storm trooper libelous because it accused him of showing "favoritism to a political party." The court ruled that, since Weiss had always acted in accordance with the orders of his superiors, he had never shown partiality to any political faction. Both Goebbels and Duerr received two months in jail for the cartoons and an additional three weeks for the articles. Because Goebbels was a member of the Reichstag, he did not serve a single day of his sentence.[15]

Goebbels and *Der Angriff* responded to these court cases in a number of ways. Since these strategies were not mutually exclusive, they were often carried out in conjunction with one another. First, the defendants would plead ignorance. Since few of the articles in the newspaper had bylines, the accused would simply claim that, although he was editor of the part of the paper in which the offending article appeared, he had not written it. Further, because of the time his job entailed at the understaffed paper, he had not even read the article before it appeared; nor did he know who had written it. Second, Goebbels and his cohorts often employed a stalling technique. Their lawyers would repeatedly ask for continuances and the accused would often fail to appear for his court date. Another alternative, at first only open to Goebbels but later to other members of *Der Angriff's* staff, was to make use of the immunity from prosecution accorded a member of the Reichstag. Even when the court managed to have this privilege revoked, it failed to make its sting felt. The Reichstag, which was willing to remove Goebbels's immunity from prosecution, refused to take away the Gauleiter's exemption from serving time in jail. The final tactic was to mount a counterattack on the pages of *Der Angriff*.[16]

The editors of the newspaper sought to use these cases for propaganda purposes. Often the paper derided the decisions of the courts, exhibiting its contempt for the machinations of the system. *Der Angriff's* response to the outcome of the case Weiss brought against the paper because of the "Danger! Rubber Clubs" articles and the two political cartoons is a good example in this regard. The author of the article "Jail for Dr. Goebbels: Does the Court Take Bernhard Weiss for a Donkey?" insisted that the name Isidor was not meant as a personal attack against the police vice president. Rather, it is symbolic of "the spirit of the rubber club democracy" Weiss represented. That Weiss "recognized" his own face in that of the donkey, the piece went on to argue, only indicated that he had a rather low opinion of his own looks. Surely, two months for "making [Weiss] look comical" was excessive, the article contended. In the end, however, the "most pitiful" aspect of the case was the fact that the court held that Weiss "looked like a donkey."[17]

Another response *Der Angriff* exhibited against judgments of the Weimar courts was to accuse the system of hypocrisy. Although the court acquitted Goebbels of a charge of libeling Reich President von Hindenburg, the staff of the paper was not satisfied. The purpose of the case—and in this the Nazis' enemies failed—was to silence the major critic of the system. In short, the suit was a violation of Goebbels's right to free speech. The paper did not point out the hypocrisy of this position or the fact that the concept of freedom of speech was totally foreign to the Nazi world view. The NSDAP was the beneficiary of the rules of the very system it chastised so frequently and promised to eliminate when it came to power.[18]

After President Hindenburg issued the "Presidential Decree Concerning Defense Against Political Excesses" in 1930 it became possible for Weimar authorities to prohibit periodicals that printed libelous attacks upon government officials. Under the law, newspapers could not be banned because of "their tendency as such," but only because of specific abuses. That is, a paper had actually to print a libelous article aimed at either a public official or the republican government before it could be banned. It could not be prohibited simply because of its political affiliation.[19]

A series of laws passed in 1931 established more specifically what constituted legal grounds for a prohibition. Periodicals could be banned for any combination of four reasons: (1) undermining the constitution, (2) attacking the "organs" of the government, (3) insulting a religious group, or (4) having "endangered public security or order." Under this law, dailies could be banned for as long as eight weeks (later reduced to four weeks) and all other periodicals for as much as six months. At first the Reich chancellor was responsible for issuing the bans, but later the power fell upon the minister of the interior.[20]

Weimar authorities made liberal use of this law. Journalist Wolfgang Bretholz held that "prohibitions upon newspapers were issued an average of twice per day" throughout the Reich. He provided more specific statistics for Prussia. In April 1931, ten prohibitions were issued; in May, eleven; and in June 1931, seventeen. These numbers include newspapers of all political persuasions. Between November 1930 and August 1932, *Der Angriff* was prohibited thirteen times. The bans, lasting from one to four weeks, totaled nineteen weeks.[21]

The final prohibition issued against *Der Angriff*, occurring in August 1932, serves as an excellent example of the grounds that constituted justification for a ban upon a newspaper. The warrant announcing the prohibition listed several articles published in the paper as grounds for legal action. The first piece listed was the lead article for the 23 August edition of the paper, "The Incomprehensible has Happened!" The article dealt with the conviction of five storm troopers for murdering a Pole in the Pomeranian town of Beuthen. The paper insisted that "if one hair on the heads of the convicted is harmed, not only will Germany be in jeopardy, but everything will simply be smashed to ruins." Weimar authorities held this statement to be a call for the violent overthrow of the republic. The following day, after the court handed down a death sentence, *Der Angriff* stated that "we find it a shame that five German freedom fighters will be murdered because of one Polish insurgent." The interior ministry ruled that the contention that "execution of a legal judgment of a German court" would constitute murder was an attack upon the Ministry of Justice, an organ of the state and, therefore, justification for a prohibition. Yet another article insisted that the court's decision had been based upon political considerations that had little to do with justice. Because this was untrue, the article was considered libelous and hence cited as further grounds for a prohibition. The ban lasted one week. The matter-of-fact manner in which Goebbels mentioned the prohibition in his diaries is indicative of the fact that, by this time, the Gauleiter had had extensive contact with the courts and took dealings with them in stride.[22]

The effectiveness of such bans is difficult to determine with certainty, but some conclusions can be safely drawn. On the negative side, the editors of *Der Angriff* saw any prohibition imposed by the system as a badge of honor. On the day in which a ban went into effect, the paper would publish a special one-page edition announcing the actions of the Interior Ministry. "*Der Angriff* verboten!" the headline would read. Beneath the headline would appear an excerpt from the police warrant ordering the ban. Not only did this provide an opportunity to show to *Der Angriff's* readers that the paper was being punished for attacking the system, it also permitted the editors to reprint the most vicious portions of the libelous copy. In short, prohibitions were counterproductive to the extent that they, like libel cases brought before the courts, provided more material for Gau Berlin's propaganda machine.[23]

Prohibitions and libel suits, however, apparently proved effective on other levels. First and foremost, prohibitions denied the editors of *Der Angriff* the opportunity to reach tens of thousands of readers every day. Bans were a serious blow to the Gau's propaganda apparatus. In addition, the paper was in almost constant financial difficulty, and a prohibition imposed additional monetary hardships. If no papers were printed, none were sold, and no money was collected from newsstand sales. Employees, however, still had to be paid, news-gathering activities had to continue, and the materials necessary to publish future editions had to be bought. By 1932, *Der Angriff* had a circulation of over one hundred thousand; hence the money lost during a week-long ban would have been significant. Also, tens of thousands of marks in fines were accrued as a result of legal actions. Although Goebbels could afford to ignore prison sentences, the Gau simply could not afford to pay these fines.

At one time Hinkel noted that, because of bans imposed by the interior ministry, *Der Angriff* was in dire straits, having enough paper for only two days and no one willing to extend the newspaper credit. The effectiveness of the legal actions brought against the Berlin organ is evinced by the reduction in the number of attacks against Weiss published in *Der Angriff* throughout 1930. By the end of the year, the hooked-nose caricatures of the vice president of the Berlin Police Force had disappeared entirely. This was likely the result of Weiss's continuous stream of libel cases brought against the paper. These cost *Der Angriff* money not only in the form of fines but also in costly legal fees. In 1930 *Der Angriff* simply capitulated in its war with the police vice president. The system won this battle.[24]

Der Angriff's battles with the system and what the paper viewed as its primary symbol, Bernhard Weiss, show much about the propaganda techniques of Gau Berlin. In the eyes of the Nazi newspaper, the system was corrupt, uncaring, and dominated by Jews. Perhaps the most important conclusion to be drawn is that at the heart of *Der Angriff* was a virulent anti-Semitism. The system was responsible for all of Germany's ills, and the Jews dominated it. In short, *Der Angriff* held the Jews responsible for all the ills plaguing Germany: inflation, unemployment, poverty, military weakness, the Versailles Treaty and reparations, as well as Marxism and class conflict. Indeed, it is possible to say that anti-Semitism was the central theme around which the staff of *Der Angriff* structured *all* of its propaganda.

This fact helps further to support the contention that the National Socialist *Weltanschauung* was the result of a radical rejection of modernity. Ultimately, anti-Semitism was not so much the rejection of a people as it was the hatred of a way of life. As historian Peter Pulzer has pointed out, as central Europe became increasingly industrialized and overpopulated, anti-Jewish views became more prevalent. Since Germany's Jewish population was concentrated in the country's urban centers (Jews were not permitted to own land), it became popular to link the Jews with all of the perceived ills inherent in urban life: industry, overcrowding, the abuses of finance capital, and the dehumanization of Germany's common people. All of these things were common themes in *Der Angriff's* propaganda, and all revolved around an anti-Semitic motif. If it can be said that ultimately all of the paper's propaganda was anti-Semitic in its origins, it follows that National Socialism was, in the end, an antimodernist movement. This is true in spite of the fact that the Nazis did not hesitate to make use of such modern propaganda tools as newspapers.[25]

The Berlin NSDAP's only goal was political power, as can be seen in the hypocritical methods *Der Angriff* used to battle the system. The Nazis were totally without scruples in this regard. When it suited them to do so, Goebbels and his underlings continually made use of a system they held was the creation of the much-hated Jews. Ironically, if not for the protection afforded by that system they could not have battled it as effectively as they did. The constitution of the Weimar Republic contained the seeds of its own destruction. On the other hand, if the Weimar Republic had not guaranteed freedom of speech, it could hardly have considered itself a republic.

Conclusion

On 30 January 1933 Adolf Hitler became chancellor of Germany, beginning a new era in European history. During the next twelve years, the Nazi regime affected the lives of millions. The changes brought by the Nazi "seizure of power" also had an effect upon *Der Angriff*. The paper was no longer a major concern to Goebbels, who became chief of the Third Reich's immense propaganda machine. It eventually fell out of his orbit, becoming the official organ of the German Labor Front. Although *Der Angriff* continued to be published until April 1945, it did not play a major role in Hitler's Germany.

But *Der Angriff* played an important part in the rise of National Socialism in Berlin. The paper was born in a period of extreme hardship for the Berlin NSDAP and helped maintain the existence of Nazism in the face a police prohibition. Many of the future leaders of Berlin's NSDAP got their start working for *Der Angriff*. For the first year of its existence the paper was the only legal means by which Goebbels could propagate Nazi ideas. For this reason, he paid special attention to the contents of the paper, always striving to create the atmosphere of a street battle or a barroom brawl. He knew that this type of nihilistic hooliganism appealed to his constituents. The Gauleiter was as successful as could have been expected given the limited resources with which he was working. Indeed, it is possible that, if Goebbels had not created a newspaper in the summer of 1927, the Berlin NSDAP may have perished.

Der Angriff continued to provide a vehicle for Nazi propaganda throughout the Kampfzeit. On its pages, Goebbels and his underlings could present their world view to the paper's readers. At first these were few in number. Later, as electoral successes mounted, circulation increased to over one hundred thousand daily, making *Der Angriff* a force to be reckoned with. It became an important actor in Berlin's political life, a serious rival to the other political newspapers published in the German capital.

The paper's propaganda methods were largely negative in character. The writers, editors, and cartoonists simply attacked the Weimar Republic and everything connected with it, offering no alternative program of their own. At the same time, the paper emphasized the Nazi contention that, once the NSDAP came to power, all of Germany's problems would be solved. These motifs had an important effect. For example, many Berliners thought that Bernhard Weiss's real name was Isidor. Further, *Der Angriff* helped make Horst Wessel a national hero. It played an important role in intra-party disputes such as the Goebbels-Strasser feud and the Stennes revolt and helped to create the Hitler Myth, which would play such a prominent role in the Third Reich.

At the core of this propaganda was a virulent anti-Semitism. The paper was consistent with the party line in blaming all of Germany's ills upon the Jews. The Jews stood behind the Weimar Republic, which the Nazis held responsible for everything bad in Germany. *Der Angriff's* anti-Semitic propaganda was unique in that it tried to appeal to Germany's proletariat. Previously, hatred of Jews was, for the most part, the dominion of peasant politics. It had made little headway within working-class movements. Even after the electoral debacle of May 1928, *Der Angriff* continued to concentrate its efforts upon the proletariat. Circumstantial evidence indicates that many, if not most, of the paper's readers were from a working-class background.

Der Angriff's constant attacks upon the Weimar system did much to discredit further the republic in the eyes of the German right wing. The economic debacle beginning in 1929 helped to increase the appeal of a newspaper that strove to assail the status quo at every turn. This served to make the Nazis more attractive to many German voters disillusioned with their lot under the republic. *Der Angriff* helped create a political atmosphere in which the NSDAP could flourish.

These conclusions have an impact upon larger issues. First, they help to explain why the Nazis ultimately succeeded. The staff of *Der Angriff* was adept at benefiting from the suffering of the German people. The paper, for the most part, accurately portrayed the daily misery experienced by millions of Germans. The organ helped the Nazis to appear sympathetic. Further, it told the German people that they were not to blame for their anguish. It was outsiders, the Jews, who were responsible. Finally, *Der Angriff* offered a simple solution to Germany's problems: give the NSDAP power. Its leaders knew that the only way to improve things was to eliminate the Jews from positions of authority. In this regard, the paper helped prepare the way for the persecution and eventual murder of millions of Europe's Jews and other "subhumans." If anti-Semitism were at the center of every aspect of Nazi ideology, it is clear that National Socialism was an anti-modernist movement. It was not the last gasp of monopoly capitalism as Marxist historians claim. It was organized racism. Nazism was a reaction to industrialization, urbanization, and the alienation felt by the common man in the modern world. Only by accepting this fact can scholars begin to understand the seemingly inexplicable phenomenon that was the Third Reich.

If one accepts the view that National Socialism was ultimately an antimodern phenomenon, this calls into question efforts to link it too closely with Marxism-Leninism. Whereas Nazism rejected industrialization and the proletarianization of much of the German population, Marxism-Leninism accepted these changes, hoping to end the "exploitation" inherent in industrial capitalism and replace it with a "humanist" alternative. In short, while it is clear that Hitler's Germany and Stalin's Soviet Union were both responsible for the deaths of millions, the motives of each regime were quite different.

This is a fact that historians, like Ernst Nolte, who try to equate the two movements ignore. National Socialism was unique.[1]

Evidence culled from *Der Angriff* makes it clear that, in contrast to what other historians have said, the NSDAP did not give up on appeals to the proletariat after May 1928. This indicates that, in spite of all its bizarre and repugnant elements, Nazi ideology had a pragmatic side. The Nazis wanted political power. If Goebbels were to succeed in Berlin, he had to concentrate his propaganda upon the city's large working-class population. He adapted his propaganda to local conditions. Further, if the Nazis really wanted to create a mythical *Volksgemeinschaft*, they would need the support of Germany's proletariat. In this respect, Goebbels was looking ahead to the years after Hitler came to power. The Gauleiter clearly believed that the Third Reich was approaching. He, with the aid of his newspaper, was able to convince tens of thousands of Berliners of this as well. This was perhaps the most important contribution that *Der Angriff* made to the rise of National Socialism in Berlin.

Notes

Introduction

1. Ernest K. Bramsted, *Goebbels and National Socialist Propaganda, 1925-1945* (East Lansing: Michigan State University Press, 1965); Jay W. Baird, *The Mythical World of Nazi War Propaganda, 1939-1945* (Minneapolis: University of Minnesota Press, 1974) and *To Die for Germany: Heroes in the Nazi Pantheon* (Bloomington: University of Indiana Press, 1990); Robert Herzstein, *The War that Hitler Won: Goebbels and the Nazi Media Campaign* (New York: Paragon House, 1978); Ian Kershaw, *The Hitler Myth: Image and Reality in the Third Reich* (Oxford: Oxford University Press, 1987) and *Popular Opinion and Political Dissent in the Third Reich: Bavaria, 1933-1945*, (Oxford: Oxford University Press, 1983); David Welch, *Propaganda and the German Cinema, 1933-1945* (Oxford: Oxford University Press, 1983); Willi A. Boelcke, ed., *Kriegspropaganda 1939-1941: Geheime Ministerkonferenzen im Reichspropagandaministerium* (Stuttgart: DTV, 1966), and *"Wollt Ihr den totalen Krieg?" Die geheimen Goebbels-konferenzen, 1939-1943* (Stuttgart: DTV, 1967). The standard work on Bolshevik propaganda techniques is Peter Kenez, *The Birth of the Propaganda State: Soviet Methods of Mass Mobilization, 1917-1929* (Cambridge: Cambridge University Press, 1985); also of interest is Nina Tumarkin's *Lenin Lives: The Lenin Cult in Soviet Russia*, (Cambridge, Mass.: Harvard University Press, 1983).

2. Oron J. Hale, *The Captive Press in the Third Reich* (Princeton: Princeton University Press, 1964); Dennis Showalter, *Little Man, What Now? "Der Stuermer" in the Weimar Republic* (New York: Greenwood Press, 1986); William L. Combs, *The Voice of the SS: A History of the SS Journal "Das Schwarze Korps"* (New York: Peter Lang, 1986); Norbert Frei and Johannes Schmitz, *Journalismus im Dritten Reich*

(Munich: C. Beck, 1989); Peter Stein, *Die NS Gaupresse, 1925-1933* (Munich: Saur, 1987). Stein lists 336 National Socialist newspapers from the Weimar period.

3. Hale, *The Captive Press in the Third Reich*, 48.

4. Hans-Georg Raehm, *"Der Angriff," 1927-1930: Der nationalsozialistische Typ der Kampfzeit* (Berlin: Eher Verlag, 1939); Helmut Heiber, *Joseph Goebbels*, (Berlin: DTV, 1962).

1. The Berlin NSDAP before *Der Angriff*, 1920-1927

1. J.K. von Engelbrechten, *Eine braune Armee entsteht* (Munich: Eher, 1937), 31.

2. Ibid., 31; Oliver C. Gleich, "Die Spandauer SA 1926 bis 1933: Eine Studie zur nationalsozialistischen Gewalt in einem Berliner Bezirk," in Wolfgang Ribbe, ed., *Berlin-Forschungen III* (Berlin [West]: Colloquium, 1988), 115; Carl Severing, *Mein Lebensweg*, vol. 1, *Vom Schlosser zum Minister* (Koeln: Greven, 1950), 426-29; Dietrich Orlow, *Weimar Prussia, 1918-1925: The Unlikely Rock of Democracy*, (Pittsburgh: University of Pittsburgh Press, 1986), 160-61.

3. Engelbrechten, *Eine braune Armee entsteht*, 32-34; *Sturm 33 Hans Maikowski: Geschrieben von Kameraden des Toten* (Berlin: Deutsch Kultur-Wacht Oscar Berger, 1940), 16; Otis Mitchell, "An Institutional History of the National Socialist SA: A Study of the SA as a Functioning Organization Within the Party Structure (1931-1934)" (Ph.D. dissertation, University of Kansas, 1964), 30.

4. Engelbrechten, *Eine braune Armee entsteht*, 36; Wolfgang Wippermann, "Aufsteig der NSDAP in Berlin," unpublished manuscript, 1.

5. Mitchell, "An Institutional History of the National Socialist SA," 35; Engelbrechten, *Eine braune Armee entsteht*, 38; Gleich, "Die Spandauer SA," 126-27.

6. See "Situations-Bericht, Juni 1926," "Situations-Bericht, Oktober 1926," in file 133, reel 5 of the NSDAP Hauptarchiv, Hoover Institution Microfilms. The early "Situations-Berichte" are also published in Martin Broszat, ed., "Die Anfaenge der Berliner NSDAP 1926/27," *Vierteljahrshefte fuer Zeitgeschichte* 8 (January 1960): 85-118; "Postscript to Situation Report of the NSDAP Concerning Spezialia 248," in Helmut Heiber, ed., *The Early Goebbels Diaries: The Journal of Joseph Goebbels from 1925-1926*, trans. by Oliver Watson (London: Weidenfeld and Nicolson, 1962), 125-26; National Socialist German Workers' Party Gau Greater Berlin to Dr. J. Goebbels, 16 October 1926, in Heiber, *The Early Goebbels Diaries*, 127.

7. Heiber, *Joseph Goebbels*, 39-45.

8. See the diary entries for 15 February, 22 February, 13 March, and 1 April 1926 in Heiber, *The Early Goebbels Diaries*, 66, 67, 68, 72, 75, concerning the incomplete nature of Goebbels's conversion.

9. Ibid., 13 April 1926, 77-78.

10. Ibid., 10, 13, 19 and 21 June 1926, 89-92.

11. Ibid., 27 and 28 August, 17 September, 18 October 1926, 107, 110, 115, and Schmiedecke to Goebbels, 28 October 1926, 129. Concerning the participation of the Berlin party in the congress see also Reinhold Muchow to Robert Duell, Neukoelln, 26 July 1926, in folder 133, reel 5, NSDAP Hauptarchiv, 1.

12. Dietrich Orlow, *The History of the Nazi Party, 1919-1933* (Pittsburgh: University of Pittsburgh Press, 1969), 92; Richard Hamilton, *Who Voted for Hitler?* (Princeton: Princeton University Press, 1982), 74; "Situations-Bericht, Oktober 1926," file 133, reel 5, NSDAP Hauptarchiv; Peter Huettenberger, *Die Gauleiter: Studie zum Wandel des Machtgefüeges in der NSDAP* (Stuttgart: Deutsche Verlag, 1969), 39-42; Gau Gross-Berlin to Dr. Joseph Goebbels, 16 October 1926, in file 199a of the Schumacher Sammlung, Bundesarchiv, Koblenz, in the Federal Republic of Germany.

13. "Situation-Bericht, Juli 1926," file 133, reel 5, NSDAP Hauptarchiv; Joseph Goebbels, *Kampf um Berlin; Der Anfang* (Munich: Eher, 1934), 24, 52; "Abschrift! Rundschreiben No. 1 der Gauleitung Berlin-Brandenburg der NSDAP," Berlin, 9 November 1926, folder 199a, Schumacher Sammlung, 1.

14. Ibid., 2; Orlow, *History of the Nazi Party*, 93; Goebbels, *Kampf um Berlin*, 21-24; "Situations-Bericht, November 1926," in file 133, reel 5, NSDAP Hauptarchiv; Viktor Reimann, *Goebbels*, trans. by Stephen Wendt (Garden City: Doubleday, 1976), 69-70.

15. Goebbels, *Kampf um Berlin*, 24-46; Bramsted, *Goebbels and National Socialist Propaganda*, 20.

16. Ibid., 26-27; "Situations-Bericht, November 1926," in file 133, reel 5, NSDAP Hauptarchiv; Orlow, *History of the Nazi Party*, 94.

17. Goebbels, *Kampf um Berlin*, 85; Engelbrechten, *Eine braune Armee entsteht*, 50.

18. Mitchell, "An Institutional History of the National Socialist SA," 40; Goebbels, *Kampf um Berlin*, 85. For information on the RFB, see Kurt G.P. Schuster, *Der Rote Frontkaempferbund, 1924-1929* (Duesseldorf: Droste, 1975).

19. Goebbels, *Kampf um Berlin*, 28; Orlow, *History of the Nazi Party*, 94; Bramsted, *Goebbels and National Socialist Propaganda*, 20.

20. Goebbels, *Kampf um Berlin*, 46; Engelbrechten, *Eine braune Armee entsteht*, 50-52.

21. Goebbels, *Kampf um Berlin*, 48-49.

22. Reimann, *Goebbels*, 72; Goebbels, *Kampf um Berlin*, 60-63.

23. Reimann, *Goebbels*, 73; Goebbels, *Kampf um Berlin*, 63-64.

24. Ibid., 64-68. Peter Longreich estimates the actual number of SA men and Communists as 800 and 200 respectively; see Peter Longreich, *Die braunen Bataillone: Geschichte der SA* (Munich: Beck, 1989), 61.

25. Goebbels, *Kampf um Berlin*, 69-72. For an excerpt from the speech see J.K. von Engelbrechten and Hans Volz, eds., *Wir wandern durch das nationalsozialistische Berlin* (Munich: Eher, 1937), 138-39.

26. Both articles are quoted at length in Goebbels, *Kampf um Berlin*, 72-73.

27. "Nationalsozialisten ueberfallen Arbeiter," in *Rote Fahne*, 12 February 1927, 1.

28. "Spezialbericht ueber die Vorgaenge auf dem Bahnhof Berlin-Lichterfelde-Ost am 20. Maerz 1927," folder 133, reel 5, NSDAP Hauptarchiv, 3-5; Goebbels, *Kampf um Berlin*, 100-102; Reimann, *Goebbels*, 78.

29. See "Spezialbericht," 6 for the route the parade took, as well as a claim that 1,800 Nazis participated. Goebbels, *Kampf um Berlin*, 102; Reimann, *Goebbels*, 78.

30. "Die Pflicht zur Verteidigung," *Rote Fahne*, 22 March 1927, 1.

31. Gleich, "Die Spandauer SA," 130.

32. Goebbels, *Kampf um Berlin*, 142-44.

33. Ibid., 144-46.

34. Ibid., 148.

35. Ibid.; Reimann, *Goebbels*, 81.

36. Goebbels, *Kampf um Berlin*, 152; "Abschrift; Der Polizeipraesident," Berlin, 5 May 1927, folder 199a, Schumacher Sammlung.

37. Goebbels, *Kampf um Berlin*, 152; Goebbels to Herrn Preussischen Innenminister Grzenski, Berlin, 6 May 1927, folder 199a, Schumacher Sammlung. For reassurances to the national organization of the NSDAP that the Berlin Nazis would not relent, see "Nationalsozialistische Deutsche Arbeiter-Partei *Berliner Irredenta*," 6 May 1927, folder 133, reel 5, NSDAP Hauptarchiv.

38. Engelbrechten, *Eine braune Armee entsteht*, 61; Goebbels, *Kampf um Berlin*, 156.

39. Ibid., 156-80.

2. An Institutional History of *Der Angriff*, 1927-1933

1. Goebbels, *Kampf um Berlin*, 187; for Lippert's account see his introduction to Hans-Georg Rahm's *"Der Angriff," 1927-1930; Der na*

tionalsozialistische Typ der Kampfzeitung (Berlin: Eher, 1939), 8-9. Lippert gives an account of conditions in the Berlin NSDAP upon the founding of *Der Angriff* in Franz Hartmann, "Die statistische und geschichtliche Entwicklung der N.S. Presse, 1926-1935" (Unpublished manuscript held in the Library of Congress, 1937), 96. This work is a manuscript compiled from the personal reminiscences of Nazi journalists and materials held in the NSDAP Hauptarchiv. Franz Hartmann was an employee of the Hauptarchiv who oversaw this project, which was never completed. See Larry Dean Wilcox, "The National Socialist Party Press in the *Kampfzeit*, 1919-1933" (Ph.D. dissertation, University of Virginia, 1970), 312.

2. Goebbels, *Kampf um Berlin*, 188; Rahm, *"Der Angriff"* 9; "Warum Angriff?" in *Der Angriff*, 4 July 1927, 1.

3. Rahm, *"Der Angriff,"* 13-18; Raymond H. Dominick III, *Wilhelm Liebknecht and the Founding of the German Social Democratic Party* (Chapel Hill: University of North Carolina Press, 1982), 255. The increased influence of the political press during the pre-war period can be seen in larger circulation. Increases in circulation are recorded in Walter Kaupert, *Die Deutsche Tagespresse als Politicum* (Freudenstadt: Oskar Kaupert, 1932), 94, 107. For example, in 1877, the SPD controlled forty-two newspapers with a circulation of 160,000; at the start of World War I, there were ninety-four Socialist papers with a combined circulation of 1,363,000.

4. On the rise in circulation experienced by the political press during the Weimar years, see Ibid., 107, 115. For example, the years 1918-1930 saw the number of Socialist organs increase from 74 to 126 (with a high of 130 in 1921 and 1926) and readership from 848,000 to 1.25 million (with a maximum of 1.7 million in 1919).

5. Roland V. Layton, "The *Voelkischer Beobachter*, 1920-1933: The Nazi Party Newspaper in the Weimar Era," *Central European History* 3 (1970): 353-82; Kaupert, *Die Deutsche Tagespresse*, 124. By 1927, seventeen regional papers had been established, nine of which still existed. See Peter Stein, *Die NS-Gaupresse*, 177; Larry D. Wilcox, "The National Socialist Party Press in the *Kampfzeit*, 1919-1933," 91-96; "Wieviele nationalsozialistische Zeitungen gibt es?" *Deutsche Presse* 21 (Number 17, 1931), 199-200. On the theoretical underpinnings of the Nazi press, see G. Stark-Berlin, *Moderne politische Propaganda* (Munich: Eher, 1930), 9-12.

6. Martin Plieninger, "Die Kampfpresse: Ein neuer Zeitungstyp," in *Zeitungswissenschaft* 2 (March 1933): 65-75; Goebbels, *Kampf um Berlin*, 192.

7. "Entwicklung der NS-Briefe," folder 1175, reel 50 of the NSDAP Hauptarchiv; Otto Strasser, *Hitler and I* (Boston: Houghton Mifflin,

1940), 84; Donald McKale, *The Nazi Party Courts: Hitler's Management of Conflict in His Movement, 1921-1945* (Lawrence: University of Kansas Press, 1974), 44-45; on the program of Strasser's group, the *Nationalsozialistische Arbeitsgemeinschaft* (NSAG), which Goebbels helped to write, see Reinhard Kuehnl, "Zur Programmatik der Nationalsozialistischen Linken: Das Strasser-Programm von 1925/26," *Vierteljahrshefte fuer Zeitgeschichte* 14 (July 1966): 317-33; pages 324-33 contain the text of the program; see also Kuehnl's *Die nationalsozialistische Linke, 1925-1930* (Meisenheim am Glan, 1966), 58-150. Kuehnl emphasizes the similarities between the Strasser and official "25 point" programs. He sees the bones of contention as the implementation of some of the leftist elements of the official program as well as a struggle for control of the movement between Hitler and Gregor Strasser.

8. See the letter dated 17 June 1927 from Koch and Hess, the "Summary" of the 10 June meeting of the Berlin NSDAP leadership and the "Summary of Charges Made at the Meeting of Officials on Friday, 10th June 1927 and Replies," in Heiber, *The Early Goebbels Diaries*, 133, 135-44; McKale, *Nazi Party Courts*, 45; Hale, *The Captive Press in the Third Reich*, 41.

9. Strasser to Hess, 15 June 1927 and Holtz to Hitler, 17 June 1927, in Heiber, *The Early Goebbels Diaries*, 132, 144-45; McKale, *Nazi Party Courts*, 46. At this time, the Kampfverlag published at least six other periodicals in addition to the BAZ. See Stein, *Die NS-Gaupresse*, 221-22.

10. McKale, *The Nazi Party Courts*, 46-48; "Der Wunsch ist der Vater des Gedankens" in *Voelkischer Beobachter*, 25 June 1927, Beilage, 3.

11. Goebbels, *Kampf um Berlin*, 197; Bramsted, *Goebbels and National Socialist Propaganda*, 30; Lippert's introduction to Rahm, *"Der Angriff,"* 9.

12. Goebbels, *Kampf um Berlin*, 196; Bramsted, *Goebbels and National Socialist Propaganda*, 30.

13. "Der Angriff: Hauptschriftleiter, Stellvertreter und Schriftleiter fuer Politik seit Gruendung bis zur Uebernahme den Zentralverlag der NSDAP," 1 and Chronology of *Der Angriff*, 1, both in folder 968, reel 47 of the NSDAP Hauptarchiv; Hartmann, "Die statistische und geschichtliche Entwicklung der NS. Presse," 94; Bramsted, *Goebbels and National Socialist Propaganda*, 30.

14. Lippert's introduction to Rahm, *"Der Angriff,"* 8; "SA-Fuehr Fragebogen," in the personnel file of Julius Lippert, Berlin Document Center.

15. Joseph Goebbels, *Die Tagebuecher von Joseph Goebbels*, ed.

by Elke Froelich (Munich: Saur, 1987), vol. 1, 23 January, 28 May and 1 September 1929, 15 March, 20 May, 1 and 3 August and 27 September 1930, 322, 377-78, 416, 515, 549, 583, 584, 609, and vol. 2, 2 January 1931, 2.

16. "Chronology of *Der Angriff*," 1; "*Der Angriff*: Hauptschriftleiter, Stellvertreter und Schriftleiter," 1; "Parteistatitische Erhebung 1939" and "Personalaufstellung," in the personnel file of Dagobert Duerr, Berlin Document Center; Rahm, *"Der Angriff,"* 29; Bramsted, *Goebbels and National Socialist Propaganda*, 30.

17. "Lebenslauf" and "Mjoelnir—ein Kampfbegriff" in the personnel file of Hans Schweitzer, Berlin Document Center; Goebbels, *Tagebuecher*, vol. 1, 7 June 1928, 231; Goebbels, *Kampf um Berlin*, 201.

18. On "Fips" see Showalter, *Little Man, What Now?* 59-68. Showalter provides numerous excellent examples of Ruprecht's work.

19. "Parteistatistische Erhebung 1939," and "Personalfragebogen," in the personnel file of Eberhard Assmann, Berlin Document Center. Unfortunately, not much information is available about Assmann. Bramsted, *Goebbels and National Socialist Propaganda*, 30; *Reichsleitung* to Melitta Wiedemann, 8 July 1931, a letter listing expulsions from the party as a result of the Stennes putsch, in the personnel file of Walther Stennes, Berlin Document Center; Gau Gross Berlin to the Reichskartei, 12 May 1931, in the personnel file of Ludwig Weissauer, Berlin Document Center. For a partial listing of members of *Der Angriff's* staff expelled after the Stennes Putsch, see the letter from Goebbels to the Geschaeftsleitung des "Angriff," 8 April 1931, in the Stennes file of the Nationalsozialistische deutsche Arbeiter-Partei; Gau Berlin collection in the Hoover Institution Archives, Stanford, California.

20. *"Hans Hinkel,"* in the Hans Hinkel Collection in the Archives of the Hoover Institution; "Hinkel, Hans," folder 1354, reel 56 of the NSDAP Hauptarchiv. On Hinkel at the *Kampfbund fuer deutsche Kultur*, see Michael Kater, "The Revenge of the Fathers: The Demise of Modern Music at the End of the Weimar Republic," *German Studies Review* 15 (May 1992): 306-7.

21. Goebbels, *Tagebuecher*, vol. 1, 19 March 1929, 22 November 1930, 345, 636, vol. 2, 27 February and 10 March 1931, 27, 31; *Reichsleitung* R.L. to Melitta Wiedemann, 8 July 1931 and Wiedemann to Hess, 12 August 1931, both in the personnel file of Walther Stennes, Berlin Document Center.

22. "Lebenslauf," "Abschrift," Letter of *Der Angriff* to unknown, 1 March 1934 and Goebbels to Reichs-und Preussischen Minister des Innern, 22 May 1939, all in the personnel file of Willi Krause, Berlin Document Center.

23. "Ausarbeitung des Pg. Karoly Kampmann" and Kampmann to NSDAP Hauptarchiv, 25 May 1937, both in file 968, reel 47 of the NSDAP Hauptarchiv.

24. "Lebenslauf," "Blatt I," "Parteistatistische Erhebung 1939," and "Auszug aus Kuerschners Deutscher Literatur-Kalender 1943," all in the personnel file of Johann von Leers, Berlin Document Center; "NSDAP, Reichsleitung, Organisationsabteilung II," 27 March 1931, folder 199a, Schumacher Sammlung, Bundesarchiv, 2.

25. Goebbels, *Kampf um Berlin*, 197; Rahm, *"Der Angriff,"* 29. For evidence that *Der Angriff* was available outside of Berlin, see the advertisement of the Buchhandlung fuer Deutsches Schrifttum in Leipzig, in file 129, box 14 of the German Subject Collection in the Hoover Institution Archives. There is, unfortunately, no record of how much of the paper's circulation was outside of Berlin or of how many firms outside the capital sold it.

26. Goebbels, *Kampf um Berlin*, 276-77; Hartmann, "Statistische und geschichtliche Entwicklung der NS.-Presse," 100-101; Rahm, *"Der Angriff,"* 67.

27. "Chronology of *Der Angriff*," and Zentral Verlag der NSDAP to NSDAP Hauptarchiv, 27 February 1936, both in the NSDAP Hauptarchiv, file 968, reel 47 of the NSDAP Hauptarchiv; Goebbels, *Kampf um Berlin*, 203, 206; Bramsted, *Goebbels and National Socialist Propaganda*, 30; *Der Angriff*, 4 July 1927.

28. Ibid., 1; Wilcox, "The National Socialist Party Press in the *Kampfzeit*," 140-41.

29. *Der Angriff*, 4 July 1927, 1-4; 11 July 1927, 3; Goebbels, *Kampf um Berlin*, 201. All of the meetings listed in the "Plakatsaeule" took place, because of the prohibition, outside of the city of Berlin.

30. *Der Angriff*, 4 July 1927, 5-8 and 28 August 1927; Wilcox, "The National Socialist Party Press in the *Kampfzeit*," 140-41.

31. *Der Angriff*, 5 September 1927, 5 and 16 January 1928, 6.

32. Goebbels, *Tagebuecher*, vol. 1, 6 January 1929, 314; *Der Angriff*, 7 and 14 January 1929.

33. "Chronology of *Der Angriff*," and Zentralverlag der NSDAP to NSDAP Hauptarchiv, 27 February 1936, both in the NSDAP Hauptarchiv, file 968, reel 47; *Der Angriff*, 3 October 1929, 6; Goebbels, *Tagebuecher*, vol. 1, 9 April 1930, 526. The letter of the Zentralverlag to the Hauptarchiv contains several inaccuracies. First, the author claimed that, as a weekly, *Der Angriff* appeared on Thursdays; it came out every Monday. In addition, he recorded that, under the semi-weekly format, it came out on Thursdays and Saturdays; it was published on Mondays and Thursdays. Finally, the letter's author recounted that *Der Angriff* became a daily in December 1930; in reality, it began daily publication on 1 November 1930. No explanation for these mistakes is

known to the author other than ignorance on the part of the composer of the letter.

34. Stein, NS-*Gaupresse*, 195; Goebbels, *Tagebuecher*, vol. 1, 2 May and 5 July 1929, 367, 395.

35. Ibid., 20 October and 5 November 1929, 442, 450.

36. Ibid., 22 November 1929, 13 January 1930, 458, 483; Rahm, "*Der Angriff,*" 152. Amann restarted publication of the Berlin edition of the *Voelkischer Beobachter* on 31 December 1932; see Stein, *Die* NS-*Gaupresse*, 195.

37. Goebbels, *Tagebuecher*, vol. 1, 31 January, 6, 9, 11, 15, 16, 18, 20 and 22 February 1930, 492, 496, 497, 498, 499, 500, 501, 503.

38. Ibid., 2, 5 and 28 April, 26 September 1930; 523, 524, 526, 537.

39. Ibid., 27 September and 15 October 1930, 609, 618; "Die Tageszeitung," in *Der Angriff*, 2 October 1930, 1.

40. Bramsted, *Goebbels and National Socialist Propaganda*, 7, 14; *Der Angriff*, 1 November 1930, 4, 8; Goebbels, *Tagebuecher*, vol. 2, 14 March 1931, 33. *Michael* was not the first serial to appear in *Der Angriff*. Beginning at the end of 1927, proletarian novels were occasionally serialized in the paper; *Michael*, however, marked the onset of a regularly published serial. In addition, since the book was the work of the organ's publisher, it received much more prominence in *Der Angriff* than previous works See Max H. Kele, *Nazis and Workers: National Socialist Appeals to German Labor, 1919-1933* (Chapel Hill: University of North Carolina Press, 1972), 111-12.

41. Goebbels, *Kampf um Berlin*, 201; Goebbels, *Tagebuecher*, vol. 1, 22 April and 1 December 1928, 1 September 1929, 217, 297, 416.

42. Roger Manvell and Heinrich Fraenkel, *Dr. Goebbels: His Life and Death* (New York: Simon and Schuster, 1960), 87-88; Goebbels, *Tagebuecher*, vol. 1, 2 and 4 December 1928, 8, 15, 22 and 23 January and 15 August 1929, 298, 299, 315, 317, 321, 322, 411.

43. Goebbels, *Kampf um Berlin*, 262.

44. Ibid., 280; Manvell and Fraenkel, *Dr. Goebbels*, 78; Goebbels, *Tagebuecher*, vol. 2, 7 January 1932, 107.

45. Ibid., vol. 1, 19 October 1928 and 20 December 1929, 279, 472.

46. Ibid., 12 November 1930, 631.

47. Ibid., 10 October and 12 November 1930, 615, 631; vol. 2, 12, 13 March 1931 and 14 December 1932, 31, 33, 305.

48. Larry D. Wilcox, "The Nazi Press before the Third Reich: *Voelkisch Presse, Kampfblaetter, Gauzeitungen*," in F.X.J. Homer and Larry D. Wilcox, eds., *Germany and Europe in the Era of the Two World Wars: Essays in Honor of Oron James Hale* (Charlottesville: University of Virginia Press, 1986), 83.

49. Hartmann, "Statistische und Geschichtliche Entwicklung der NS. Presse," 5; Goebbels, *Tagebuecher*, vol. 1, 11 November 1928, 5 January and 20 October 1929, 286, 313, 442.

50. Engelbrechten and Volz, *Wir wandern durch das nationalsozialistische Berlin*, 46; Juergen W. Falter, "Wahlen und Waehlerverhalten unter besonderer Beruecksichtigung des Aufsteiges der NSDAP nach 1928," in Karl Dietrich Bracher, Manfred Funke, and Hans-Adolf Jacobsen, eds., *Die Weimarer Republik, 1918-1933: Politik, Wirtschaft, Gesellschaft* (Duesseldorf: Droste, 1987), 486; Thomas Childers, *The Nazi Voter: The Social Foundations of Fascism in Germany, 1919-1933* (Chapel Hill: University of North Carolina Press, 1983), 119-92. For results in Berlin see Hamilton, *Who Voted for Hitler?*, 64-100.

51. Engelbrechten and Volz, *Wir wandern durch das nationalsozialistische Berlin*, 46; Hartmann, "Statistische und Geschichtliche Entwicklung der NS. Presse," 496, 503, 504; Falter, "Wahlen und Waehlerverhalten unter besonderer Beruecksichtigung des Aufsteigs der NSDAP nach 1928," 486; Goebbels, *Tagebuecher*, vol. 2, 12 March 1931, 32. When *Der Angriff's* circulation was at its zenith the readers of the *Voelkischer Beobachter* numbered approximately 120,000.

52. Jeremy R. S. Brown, "The Berlin NSDAP in the *Kampfzeit*," in *German History* 7 (August 1989): 241-47; Peter D. Stachura, "The Political Strategy of the Nazi Party, 1919-1933," in *German Studies Review* 3 (May 1980): 275-278; Michael Kater, *The Nazi Party: A Social Profile of Members and Leaders, 1919-1945* (Cambridge: Harvard University Press, 1983), 35-36. The number of upper-class readers of *Der Angriff* was probably negligible; it simply was not the type of paper that a wealthy, educated person, who had a stake in assuring the survival of capitalism, would read.

3. The Party, the Fuehrer Myth, and the Presidential Election

1. Alan Bullock, *Hitler, A Study in Tyranny*, Completely Revised Edition (New York: Harper Torchbooks, 1964), 139-40; Kele, *Nazis and Workers*, 107; Kuehnl, *Die nationalsozialistische Linke*, 146.

2. See Strasser, *Hitler and I*, 94-95, concerning Goebbels's refusal to give the BAZ information concerning Gau meetings. Although Strasser is a dubious source—he claims that *Der Angriff* was a daily in 1927—the copy published in the *Berliner Arbeiter Zeitung* supports his contention; McKale, *Nazi Party Courts*, 84; Manvell and Fraenkel, *Dr. Goebbels*, 78; Mitchell, "An Institutional History of the National Socialist SA," 42.

3. Kuehne, *Die nationalsozialistische Linke*, 148; Kele, *Nazis and Workers*, 107.

4. Stachura, "The Political Strategy of the Nazi Party," 277-81; the best account of the election of 1928 and its effects upon the NSDAP is Peter D. Stachura, "Der Kritische Wendepunkt? Die NSDAP und die Reichstagwahlen vom 20. Mai 1928," *Vierteljahrshefte fuer Zeitgeschichte* 26 (1978): 66-99; McKale, *Nazi Party Courts*, 84; Joachim C. Fest, *Hitler: Eine Biographie* (Frankfurt/M: Ullstein, 1973), 376; Peter Stachura, *Gregor Strasser and the Rise of Nazism* (London: Allen and Unwin, 1983), 77-78. Gregor Strasser did an excellent job as Organization Leader. Under his auspices, the number of party members reached 100,000 by the end of 1928; see Toland, *Adolf Hitler*, 245.

5. McKale, *Nazi Party Courts*, 72. Unfortunately, Otto's is the only existing account of his meeting with Hitler; see Strasser, *Hitler and I*, 95-98.

6. McKale, *Nazi Party Courts*, 84-85; Goebbels, *Tagebuecher*, vol. 1, 1 April 1930, 522; Strasser, *Hitler and I*, 99.

7. Quoted in Toland, *Adolf Hitler*, 251; McKale, *Nazi Party Courts*, 84; Goebbels, *Tagebuecher*, vol. 1, 30 April 1930, 539. Once again, the only recorded account of the May meetings between Strasser and Hitler are in Strasser's *Hitler and I*, 100-114. Concerning Gregor Strasser's relinquishing of authority at the Kampfverlag, see Stachura, *Gregor Strasser and the Rise of Nazism*, 77.

8. On Gregor Strasser's resignation from the Kampfverlag see "Anordnung," in *Der Angriff*, 6 July 1930, 1; the same announcement was published under the title "Erklaerung," in the *Voelkischer Beobachter*, 6-7 July 1930, 1. On Gregor's support for Hitler see Gregor Strasser to Zahnarzt Erckmann, 7 August 1930, ED 188, Sammlung Otto Strasser, Institut fuer Zeitgeschichte, Munich, in the Federal Republic of Germany; "Gregor Strasser stellt sich zu Hitler," in the *Voelkischer Beobachter*, 5 July 1930, 2, and Stachura, *Gregor Strasser and the Rise of Nazism*, 79-80 On the 2 July meeting, see "Ein Brief des Fuehrers," in *Der Angriff*, 3 July 1930, 1, and "Ein Brief Hitlers an die Berliner Gauleitung," in the *Voelkischer Beobachter*, 4 July 1930, 2. See also Stachura, *Gregor Strasser and the Rise of Nazism*, 79. For Strasser's account see Strasser, *Hitler and I*, 115-16. On the blow to radicalism in the NSDAP that the Hitler-Strasser debate delivered, see Peter Stachura, "The Nazis, the Bourgeoisie and the Workers during the *Kampfzeit*," in Peter Stachura, ed., *The Nazi Machtergreifung* (London: Allen and Unwin, 1983), 25; Wolfgang Horn, *Der Marsch zur Machtergreifung: Die NSDAP bis 1933* (Duesseldorf: Droste, 1972), 261-63.

9. See the three letters from Otto Strasser to Zahnarzt Erckmann dated 18 July, 13 August and 22 October 1930 in ED 188, Sammlung Strasser, vol. 30; Otto-Ernst Schueddekopf, *Nationalbol*

schewismus in Deutschland, 1918-1933 (Frankfurt/M: Ullstein, 1972), 325-27. There were only about 2,000-2,500 members by the end of 1930. The Berlin SA revolt of April/May 1931 caused a sudden influx of members which only had temporary benefit. For all intents and purposes, the Kampfgemeinschaft no longer existed by the beginning of 1932. Orlow, *History of the Nazi Party*, 210; Horn, *Der Marsch zur Machtergreifung*, 263.

10. "'Knueppelt sie nieder!'" in *Rote Fahne*, 5 July 1930, 1-2.

11. "Der ewige Kritikaster," *Der Angriff*, 6 July 1930, 1.

12. "Das politische Tagebuch, 2 Juli," *Der Angriff*, 6 July 1930, 3.

13. See chapter five.

14. See chapter two.

15. "Wir kapitulieren nicht!" *Der Angriff*, 1 August 1927, 1-2.

16. "Der Aufmarsch der Hunderttausend in Nuernberg" and "'Trotz Verbot—nicht tot!'" *Der Angriff*, 22 August 1927, 1. Because of the prohibition, those Berlin SA men who attended the meeting were officially members of the Brandenburg SA.

17. "Ins neue Jahr!" *Der Angriff*, 2 January 1928, 1-2. On the Nazi practice of comparing themselves to early Christians, see Charles Bracelen Flood, *Hitler: The Path to Power* (Boston: Houghton Mifflin, 1989), 261-62, 279-80, 381. Flood contends that as early as 1922, Hitler consistently compared himself to Christ and his followers to Christians. On Goebbels's efforts to turn setbacks to his own advantage, see Baird, *To Die for Germany*, 73-74.

18. *Der Angriff*, 22 August 1927, 1; and 5 March 1928, 5.

19. "Die beste Abwehr ist 'der Angriff!'" *Der Angriff*, 29 August 1927, 1, and "Der Kampf um das Verbot," 19 December 1927, 7.

20. Heiber, *Joseph Goebbels*, 68. The Nazis, needless to say, were not appreciative of Zoergiebel's decision. The lifting of the prohibition, according to *Der Angriff*, was entirely the work of Gau Berlin; see "Nach der Aufhebung des Verbotes," *Der Angriff*, 9 April 1928, 4; Goebbels, *Tagebuecher*, vol. 1, 14 April 1928; "Politisches Tagebuch" for 14 April, *Der Angriff*, 23 April 1930, 3. In German, the poem reads: "Im Streite zur Seite ist/Gott uns gestanden./Er wollte, es sollte das/ Recht siegreich sein."

21. "Warum sind wir Nationalisten?" *Der Angriff*, 9 July 1928, 1.

22. "Warum sind wir Sozialisten?" *Der Angriff*, 16 July 1928, 1.

23. "Warum sind wir Judengegner?" *Der Angriff*, 30 July 1928, 1-2.

24. On Hitler's use of his charismatic personality to seize control of the Nazi Party see Orlow, *History of the Nazi Party*, 20-38; on the "Fuehrer myth" in the Weimar Republic, see Kershaw, *The "Hitler Myth"*, 13-47.

25. *Der Angriff*, 23 April 1928, 1.

26. "Das Bild des Fuehrers," *Der Angriff*, 22 August 1927, 1; and 29 August 1927, 5

27. "Adolf Hitler spricht!" *Der Angriff*, 16 July 1928, 4. Neither this article nor Goebbels's diaries name the hall in which the assembly was held.

28. "Italienisches Press-Echo zur Berliner Hitlerrede," *Der Angriff*, 6 August 1928, 4.

29. "Hitler—ein Jude!" *Der Angriff*, 30 January 1928, 4.

30. Erich Eyck, *A History of the Weimar Republic*, vol. 2, *From the Locarno Conference to Hitler's Seizure of Power* (Cambridge: Harvard University Press, 1963), 350-53.

31. Andreas Dorpalen, *Hindenburg and the Weimar Republic* (Princeton: Princeton University Press, 1964), 256-60; Gottfried Reinhold Treviranus, *Das Ende von Weimar: Heinrich Bruening und seine Zeit* (Duesseldorf: Econ, 1968), 299; Heinrich Bruening, *Memoiren, 1918-1934* (Stuttgart: Deutsche Verlaganstalt, 1970), 533; Eyck, *History of the Weimar Republic*, vol. 2, 360, 355. For Nazi conjectures regarding whether or not Hindenburg would run, see Goebbels, *Tagebuecher*, vol. 2, 12 January 1932, 109.

32. William L. Shirer, *The Rise and Fall of the Third Reich: A History of Nazi Germany* (New York: Fawcett, 1959), 219.

33. Joseph Goebbels, *Vom Kaiserhof zur Reichskanzlei* (Munich: Eher Verlag, 1938), 21 January, 2 February and 22 February 1932, 27-28, 35-37, 49-50; Goebbels, *Tagebuecher*, vol. 2, 19, 26 January, 3 February, 1932, 111-12, 116, 120-21; "Spontane Huldigung im Sportpalast fuer Adolf Hitler," *Der Angriff*, 30 January 1932, 1.

34. Flugblaetter numbers 33, 34, 36a in Akten 2088, Repositorium 240 in the Landesarchiv Berlin, Berlin, Federal Republic of Germany; Flugblatt number 84, file 199 in Akten XII, Hauptarchiv IV, Geheimes Staatsarchiv preussischer Kulturbesitz, Berlin, Federal Republic of Germany. For a brief overview of the entire campaign, see Karl Dietrich Bracher, *Die Aufloesung der Weimarer Republik* (Duesseldorf: Droste, 1955), 414-18.

35. Guenter Hortzschansky, Walter Wimmer, Lothar Berthold, Heinz Karl, Horst Naumann and Stefan Weber, *Ernst Thaelmann: Eine Biographie* (East Berlin: Dietz, 1980), 551-61; Flugblatt number 92, file 199, Akten XII Hauptarchiv IV, Geheimes Staatsarchiv preussischer Kulturbesitz. Unfortunately, there is not much information available about Duesterberg's campaign.

36. Reichspropagandaleitung der N.S.D.A.P., "*Sonderrundschreiben an alle Gaue und Gaupropaganda-leitungen*," file 287, reel 15 of the NSDAP Hauptarchiv.

37. Goebbels, *Vom Kaiserhof zur Reichskanzlei*, 7 January 1932, 20; Otto Wagener, *Hitler, Memoirs of a Confidant*, edited and translated by Henry Asheby Turner. Jr (New Haven: Yale University Press, 1985), 184.

38. "Appell an die, die es angeht," *Der Angriff*, 23 January 1932, 1-2.

39. *Der Angriff*, 15 February 1932, 1; and 23 February, 1. Nazi election posters also emphasized these themes. See the posters in file 287, reel 15 of the NSDAP Hauptarchiv.

40. "Neuer Sturm im Reichstag," *Der Angriff*, 25 February 1932, 1; "SPD.—ein Organ des Staates?" in 5 March 1932, 2; "Blamable 'Front' um Hindenburg," 7 March 1932, 1.

41. "Berlins Arbeiter waehlen Adolf Hitler!" *Der Angriff*, 10 March 1932, 4.

42. "Schluss jetzt! Deutschland waehlt Hitler," in *Der Angriff*, special election edition published at the end of February, 1.

43. Goebbels, *Tagebuecher*, vol. 2, 13 March 1932, 140; Engelbrechten and Volz, *Wir wandern durch das nationalsozialistische Berlin*, 48; Bracher, *Aufloesung der Weimarer Republik*, 418-19; Eyck, *History of the Weimar Republic*, vol. 2, 360-61.

44. "Volksmehrheit gegen Hindenburg; NSDAP. fast verdoppelt" and "Nationalsozialistische Stimmen Berlins verdoppelt," *Der Angriff*, 14 March 1932, 1, 4; and "Unser Einbruch in die gegnerische Front," 15 March 1932, 2.

45. "*Anordnung* fuer *die Werbeaktion der nationalsozialistischen Presse fuer den 2.Wahlgang [sic] zur Reichspraesidentenwahl*," 23 March 1932, file 289, reel 15 of the NSDAP Hauptarchiv, 1-2.

46. "Von Lenin zu Adolf Hitler," *Der Angriff*, 22 March 1932, 6.

47. "Stahlhelmfuehrer fuer Hitler Der nationale Einheitskandidat," *Der Angriff*, 31 March 1932, 1.

48. "Hitler, der politische Kaempfer," *Der Angriff*, 31 March 1932, 1.

49. "Start zum Deutschlandflug," *Der Angriff*, 4 April 1932, 1; Childers, *The Nazi Voter*, 197.

50. "80 000 in Dresden," *Der Angriff*, 4 April 1932, 1-2; "60 000 in Potsdam," 5 April 1932, 2; and "Vor 50 000 Pommern Grenzlandkundgebung in Lauenburg," 6 April 1932, 1.

51. "Adolf Hitler als Mensch" and "Wir Brandenburger gruessen den Fuehrer," *Der Angriff*, 4 April 1932, 5, 8; "Adolf Hitler als Kamerad," 2 April 1932, 3.

52. "Adolf Hitler bringt Chaos, Buergerkrieg und Inflation," *Der Angriff*, 4 April 1932, 3; "*Adolf Hitler*: Mein Program," 5 April 1932, 5; "40 000 Nuernberger umjubeln den Fuehrer," 7 April 1932,

2. On Nazi appeals to German women, see Claudia Koonz, *Mothers in the Fatherland: Women, the Family and Nazi Politics* (New York: St. Martins, 1987), 19-91.

53. "Hitler's gewaltiger Sieg," *Der Angriff*, 11 April 1932, 1; Engelbrechten and Volz, *Wir wandern durch das nationalsozialistische Berlin*, 48; Hortschansky, et al., *Ernst Thaelmann*, 562.

54. Bracher, *Die Aufloesung der Weimarer Republik*, 460-61.

4. The SA and Political Violence

1. On *Der Stuermer* see, Showalter, *Little Man, What Now?*

2. Engelbrechten, *Eine braune Armee entsteht*, 39, 73, 120-23, 164, 253. Engelbrechten's numbers are, as always, questionable sources, but the only ones available.

3. Michael H. Kater, "Ansaetze zu einer Soziologie der SA bis zur Roehm-Krise," in Ulrich Engelhardt, Volker Sellin, Horst Stuke, eds., *Soziale Bewegung und politische Verfassung: Beitraege zur Geschichte der modernen Welt* (Stuttgart: Ernst Klett, 1976), 801. Kater's statistics concerning class composition of the SA differ significantly from those of Peter Merkl. They agree, however, that, compared with the party organization, the working classes were overrepresented in the SA. Merkl's conclusions are based upon a larger sample (581) than Kater's (160); but Kater's sample is from the industrial city of Essen, and therefore more likely representative of Berlin. Conan Fischer's conclusions, based upon a sample of 1,312 storm troopers, are closer to Kater's than Merkl's, at 62.6 percent of storm troopers from a proletarian background. See Peter H. Merkl, *The Making of a Stormtrooper* (Princeton: Princeton University Press, 1980), 99; and Conan Fischer, *Stormtroopers: A Social, Economic and Ideological Analysis* (London: George Allen and Unwin, 1983), 26. Concerning the percentage of working-class members of the NSDAP during the "years of struggle," see Kater, *The Nazi Party*, 34-38, 52-55.

4. Fischer, *Stormtroopers*, 46. On the SA *Heime* and the attraction of violence to storm troopers, see Richard Bessel, *Political Violence and the Rise of Nazism: The Storm Troopers in Eastern Germany, 1925-1934* (New Haven: Yale University Press, 1984), 49-53, 75-96

5. See numerous cartoons depicting SA men on the pages of *Der Angriff*; for example "Die letzte Vision" and "Warum sind wir Nationalisten," both in *Der Angriff*, 7 November 1927, 1 and 9 June 1928, 1 respectively. On the NSDAP's care for storm troopers, see "S.A. Versicherung und S.A.-Staerke in Berlin," in *Der Angriff*, 20 February 1930, 4. On cultural and sporting opportunities provided by the SA aimed at occupying the time of unemployed storm troopers, see

"S.A.-Sport und Kultur—eine Einheit," in *Der Angriff*, 23 February 1930, 4.

6. "Pg. Ernst Schwartz zum Gedaechtnis!" in *Der Angriff*, 22 January 1931, 6.

7. See the series of articles appearing on the sports page of *Der Angriff*, entitled "Jeder 'Angriff'—Leser wird Boxer." For an overview of paramilitary politics in the Weimar Republic, see James M. Diehl, *Paramilitary Politics in Weimar Germany* (Bloomington: Indiana University Press, 1977).

8. "Ueberall Blutterror kommunistischer Verbrecherbanden," in *Der Angriff*, 30 April 1928, 4.

9. See numerous cartoons representing the Jews as being behind attacks upon the SA; for example, "Heilige Opfer" and "Drei gemeuchelte Nationalsozialisten in zwei Tagen!" in *Der Angriff*, 23 January 1930, 5 and 21 January 1931, 1 respectively. On clashes between working-class members of the various paramilitary groups, see "'Arbeiter' gegen Arbeiter," *Der Angriff*, 26 January 1930, 6.

10. On the RFB "campaign against the SA-taverns," which came to a climax in 1931, see Eve Rosenhaft, *Beating the Fascists? The German Communists and Political Violence, 1929-1933* (Cambridge: Cambridge University Press, 1983), 111-27. For an account of political violence in Berlin from the Communists' point of view, see James J. Ward, "'Smash the Fascists . . . ' German Communist Efforts to Counter the Nazis, 1930-1931," *Central European History* 14 (March 1981): 30-62. Anklageschrift gegen Erich Henschel, Repositorium 58, Aktum 108 in the Landesarchiv Berlin, Berlin, Germany, 6, 14-15, 108. Herschel, a Nazi worker, received three months in jail for assault.

11. "Blutige Schlacht in Schoeneberg," *Der Angriff*, 26 September 1927, 4.

12. On the Berlin NSDAP's attitude toward the police, see also Goebbels, *Das Buch Isidor*.

13. Concerning the number of SA men killed throughout the Reich before September 1932, see *Halbmast: Ein Heldenbuch der SA. und SS.* (Berlin: Verlag Braune Buecher, 1932), 9. The number given there is somewhat inflated, in that it includes members of paramilitary groups that were precursors of the SA as well as SS men and members of the Hitler Youth. The number of storm troopers killed in Berlin between 1926 and August 1932 was found by counting the number listed in *Halbmast* on pages 29-32, 44-48, 58-72. During this same period, three Hitler Youths and one SS man were also killed. For storm troopers as "holy sacrifices," see, for example, the cartoon "Heilige Opfer," in *Der Angriff*, 23 January 1930, 5. The poem

"Zweihundert sind tot . . . " can be found in *Der Angriff*, 22 January 1931, 6. It reads in German: "Sie haben gekaempft bei Tag und in dunkler Nacht,/Sie haben zweihundert Tote zu Grabe gebracht,/Sie haben gelitten und dennoch niemals gezagt,/Und haben gestritten und immer nur Eines gesagt:/ Zweihundert sind tot, aber Hunderttausende stehen,/Weil Deutschland nicht fallen darf und nicht untergeh'n./Sie haben gekaempft fuer den neuen, den kommenden Staat,/Sie hielten zusammen trotz Terror und Tod und Verrat,/Sie halten die Fahne und liessen sie nicht mehr los/Und halten sie fest, bis Deutschland frei ist und gross./Zweihundert sind tot, doch die rauschenden Fahnen weh'n,/Weil Deutschland nicht fallen darf und nicht untergeh'n.'

14. *Halbmast*, 51; Engelbrechten, *Eine braune Armee entsteht*, 110-11; Engelbrechten and Volz, *Wir wandern durch das nationalsozialistische Berlin*, 218-19.

15. "Der Tote," in *Der Angriff*, 19 January 1929, 1.

16. Ibid.

17. For the best account of the creation of the Horst Wessel myth, see Baird, *To Die for Germany*, 73-107. Concerning the film about Wessel's life and death, see Welch, *Propaganda and the German Cinema*, 75-87.

18. Baird, *To Die For Germany*, 75-80; *Halbmast*, 24-25; Engelbrechten, *Eine braune Armee entsteht*, 92-93. See also the pamphlet, *Horst Wessel: knappe sein—heisst: treu sein—wahr sein Kaempfer sein* (Leipzig: Die nationale Aufbau, n.d.), *passim*; Wilfred Bade, *Die S.A. erobert Berlin* (Munich: Verlag Knorr und Hirth, 1933), 173-177. Concerning Wessel becoming *Sturmfuehrer* see, Irme Lazar, *Der Fall Horst Wessel* (Stuttgart: Belser Verlag, 1980), 70-79.

19. Baird, *To Die for Germany*, 79-80; Lazar, *Der Fall Horst Wessel*, 96-99 For the KPD's version of events, see "SA.-Fuehrer aus Eifersucht umgelegt," "Nazistudent Wessel war ein Zuhaelter," "'Der beste Sturmfuehrer' ein Zuhaelter," all in *Rote Fahne*, 16, 18 and 21 January 1930, 8, 7 and 10 respectively.

20. Baird, *To Die for Germany*, 80; Goebbels, *Tagebuecher*, vol. 1, 23 February 1930, 503-4. Anticipating the creation of the "resurrection myth" surrounding Wessel, Goebbels referred to him as "a wanderer between two worlds." Horst's brother, Werner, who was also a storm trooper, had died in a skiing accident in December 1929. See "Mein Kamerad," *Der Angriff*, 5 January 1930, 6.

21. "Die Bluttat an dem Sturmfuehrer Wessel," in *Der Angriff*, 19 January 1930, 4. In fact, Hoehler was sent to Prague.

22. "Horst Wessel and die Giftbrut im Liebknecht-Haus," in *Der Angriff*, 23 January 1930, 4.

23. "Heilige Opfer," *Der Angriff*, 23 January 1930, 5.

24. "Horst Wessel als Sieger," *Der Angriff*, 13 March 1930, 4. Unfortunately, the issues dealing with Wessel's death and burial have not been microfilmed.

25. See the police file in Repositorium 58, Aktum 37 of the Landesarchiv Berlin, vol. 1, 3. Because of conflicting stories given by each side, the police often had difficulty in determining exactly what happened. In addition, whenever the police reached the scene of one of these brawls, they were quick to use their weapons. Policemen were in danger from both sides. *Halbmast*, 58; Engelbrechten and Volz, *Wir wandern durch das nationalsozialistische Berlin*, 149-50.

26. "Die Beisetzung des Truppfuehrers Pg. Schwartz," *Der Angriff*, 25 January 1932, 3. For a picture of storm troopers carrying Schwartz's coffin to this grave, see "Wir trugen Kamerad Schwartz zu Grabe," *Der Angriff*, 29 January 1932, 7.

27. "Augenzeugen berichten ueber den Meuchelmord von Reinickendorf," *Der Angriff*, 20 January 1932, 11.

28. Ibid.

29. On Norkus and Nazi propaganda, see Baird, *To Die for Germany*, 108-29. The death of Norkus was also the subject of a propaganda film during the first years of the Third Reich. See Welch, *Propaganda and the German Cinema*, 59-74.

30. See Repositorium 58, Aktum 9 in the Landesarchiv Berlin, vol. 1, 6. Much of this account is based upon a statement by Kirsch. Baird, *To Die for Germany*, 114-15.

31. Ibid, 115.

32. "Der Meuchelmord an dem Hitlerjungen" and "Wie der Hitlerjunge Herbert Norkus gemeuchelt wurde," *Der Angriff*, 25 January, 1932, 1, 9.

33. "Die Hintermaenner des feigen Meuchelmordes," in *Der Angriff*, 25 January 1932, 9.

34. "Du toter Kamerad!" *Der Angriff*, 26 January 1932, 4. On the KPD's alleged persecution of Norkus's father and its effects upon Herbert, see "Der Vater," in *Der Angriff*, 26 January 1932, 4.

35. This quotation is taken from Baird, *To Die for Germany*, 116.

36. For accounts of the two Stennes revolts—there was also one in August-September 1930—see Engelbrechten, *Eine braune Armee entsteht*, 138-39; Orlow, *History of the Nazi Party*, 217-20; Sauer, *Die Mobilmachung der Gewalt*, 217-18; Mitchell, "An Institutional History of the National Socialist SA," 74-75; Longreich, *Die braunen Bataillone*, 103-11; Thomas Childers and Eugene Weiss, "Voters and Violence: Political Violence and the Limits of National Socialist Mass Mobilization," in *German Studies Review* 12 (October 1990):

486. For brief accounts of Goebbels's actions during the rebellions, see Heiber, *Joseph Goebbels*, 91-93, and Werner, "SA und NSDAP," 529-30.

37. "Rechtsradikale Bewegung: N.S.D.A.P.: Die Stennes Revolte," Report of the Landeskriminalpolizei (IA) of Berlin, 1 May 1931, 7, in the personal file of Walther Stennes, Berlin Document Center; Alfred Krebs, *The Infancy of Nazism*, W.S. Allen, ed. (New York: Watts, 1976), 202-3.

38. Longreich, *Die braunen Bataillone*, 103; Mitchell, "An Institutional History of the National Socialist SA," 37-38. See also Goebbels's diary entry for 12 August 1930 in his *Tagebuecher*, vol. 1, 588-89; Horn, *Der Marsch zur Machtergreifung*, 326. Heinz Hoehne holds that the motives of the mutineers can be seen primarily in the growing conflict between the SA and SS. While this may have been a contributing factor, the evidence makes it clear that it was not as important as those presented above. See Heinz Hoehne, *The Order of the Death's Head: The Story of Hitler's SS*, trans. Richard Barry (New York: Ballantine, 1969), 71-77.

39. On the Berlin SA see Mitchell, "An Institutional History of the National Socialist SA," 38 and Longreich, *Die braunen Bataillone*, 111. Regarding Stennes's biography see F.L. Carsten, *The Rise of Fascism* (Berkeley: University of California Press, 1967), 168, and Schueddekopf, *Nationalbolshewismus in Deutschland*, 517. On the putsch of the "Black Reichswehr," see F.L. Carsten, *The Reichswehr and Politics 1918-1933*, (Berkeley: University of California Press, 1973), 168-69.

40. Goebbels, *Tagebuecher*, vol. 1, 30 August 1930, 595; "Pg! SA-Kameraden," Berlin, 1 September 1930, file 315, reel 17 of the NSDAP Hauptarchiv.

41. Heiber, *Joseph Goebbels*, 91; Goebbels, *Tagebuecher*, vol. 1, 1 September 1930, 596-97; Bessel, *Political Violence and the Rise of Nazism*, 62-63; Fest, *Hitler*, 395. Concerning the clash between the SA and SS as well as the roots of the growing enmity between the two organizations see Michael Kater, "Zum gegenseitigen Verhaeltnis von SA und SS in der Sozialgeschichte des Nationalsozialismus von 1925 bis 1933," in *Vierteljahrschrift fuer Sozial-und Wirtschaftlichgeschichte* 62 (1975): 348. On the revolutionary outlook of large portions of the SA see Werner, "SA und NSDAP," 524.

42. For Goebbels as head of the SA see "Rundschreiben No. 1 der Gauleitung Berlin-Brandenburg der N.S.D.A.P.;" Orlow, *History of the Nazi Party*, 93.

43. Goebbels, *Tagebuecher*, vol. 1, 21 September and 18 December 1930, 606, 647; vol. 2, 11 and 20 January 1931, 6, 10; Kater, "Zum gegenseitigen Verhaeltnis von SA und SS," 341-54. Goebbels also had friendly meetings with Stennes on 22 January and 21 February 1931.

See his diary entries for 23 January and 23 February 1931 in *Tagebuecher*, vol. 2, 11 and 25. In general, it can be said that Goebbels's animosity toward the Munich leadership was the product of the Gauleiter's contention that Munich did not put enough effort into winning support in Germany's northern cities.

44. Goebbels, *Tagebuecher*, vol. 1, 2 October and 28 November 1930, 612, 637-638. The leadership of the SA was organized in a hierarchical manner. The national leader was the Osaf, underneath him was a regional leader and then a chief of the SA on the Gau level.

45. Mitchell, "An Institutional History of the National Socialist SA," 61; Bessel, *Political Violence and the Rise of Nazism*, 63; "Erlass Nr. 2," Munich, 20 February 1931, file 306, reel 16 of the NSDAP Hauptarchiv.

46. Stennes to Roehm, 28 February 1931, file 325, reel 17 of the NSDAP Hauptarchiv. For an excellent example of the reaction of the Berlin rank and file see "Pg.! SA Kameraden!" Berlin, 25 February 1931, file 322, reel 17 of the NSDAP Hauptarchiv.

47. Goebbels, *Tagebuecher*, vol. 2, 16 March 1931, 34.

48. Ibid., 31 March 1931, 42; "Rechtsradikale Bewegung," 7.

49. Jahn's account is quoted in Werner, "SA und NSDAP," 529; Goebbels, *Tagebuecher*, vol 2, 31 March 1931, 42.

50. Ibid., 2 April 1931, 42; Werner, "SA und NSDAP," 530. Concerning Goebbels's speeches in Dresden see *Der Angriff* for 1 April 1931, 1. For claims that Goebbels had sold out Stennes see Heiden, *Der Fuehrer*, 372 and Orlow, *History of the Nazi Party*, 217, fn 158. Orlow bases his conclusions upon Krebs's memoirs. On the delegation to Goebbels see Heiber, *Joseph Goebbels*, 93.

51. Goebbels, *Tagebuecher*, vol. 2, 2 April 1931, 42-43; Werner, "SA und NSDAP," 530; Mitchell, "An Institutional History of the National Socialist SA," 74-75. On Stennes and *Der Angriff* see "Der missglueckte Stennesputsch auf den 'Angriff,'" in the *Voelkischer Beobachter* for 4 April 1931, 7. See also *Der Angriff* for 1 and 2 April 1931. For the removal of Goebbels from his Gau leader post see the leaflet, "Nationalsozialisten Berlins!" file 325, reel 17 of the NSDAP Hauptarchiv.

52. Schuddekopf, *Nationalbolshewismus in Deutschland*, 328; "Rechtsradikale Bewegung," 6. Concerning the Stennes revolt outside of Berlin see Bessel, *Political Violence and the Rise of Nazism*, 62-65.

53. "Pg., SA Kameraden! Nationalsozialisten!" Berlin, 8 April 1931, file 322, reel 17 of the NSDAP Hauptarchiv; "Einigung um Stennes?" and "Wir kaempfen um unsere Idee: Es geht um Deutschland!" in *Der Angriff*, 2 April 1931, 1, 6.

54. "Nationalsozialistische Kampfbewegung Deutschlands: Organisationsbefehl Nr. 1," Berlin, 7 May 1931, file 325, reel 17 of

THE NSDAP Hauptarchiv; Schuddekopf, *Nationalbolschewismus in Deutschland*, 304, 327-28. That not all of the insurgents followed Stennes into the NSKD is indicative of the popular feeling that Stennes's organization had little chance for success.

55. For accusations against Goebbels see his *Tagebuecher*, vol. 2, 4 and 6 April 1931, 43-44. Concerning the Gauleiter's health, see the entry for 11 April 1931, 46. For police expectations that Goebbels would be replaced see "Rechtsradikale Bewegung," 7-8. The police go so far as to name his likely successor, Hans Hinkel.

56. Goebbels, *Tagebuecher*, vol. 2, 2 April 1931, 42; "Adolf Hitler fordert: Scharfster Kampf gegen Saboteure in der N.S.D.A.P.," *Voelkischer Beobachter*, 3 April 1931, 9.

57. In his diary, Goebbels states that Amann wanted the newspaper to be eight pages. The fact that it was only reduced to ten pages is further evidence of Goebbels's continued influence over the newspaper. See Goebbels, *Tagebuecher*, vol. 2, 9, 14, 21, 25 April 1931, 45, 48, 53, 55; 3, 10, 17 and 19 June 1931, 73, 76, 80, 81.

58. "Rechtsradikale Bewegung," 7-8; Goebbels, *Tagebuecher*, vol. 2, 22 and 28 April 1931, 54, 56.

59. Goebbels, *Tagebuecher*, vol. 2, 9, 11, 17, 21 April 1931, 45, 46, 50, 53. For journalistic attacks upon Stennes see *Der Angriff* for 4 April 1931, 1, 4. For Goebbels's speech to the SA see the diary entry for 17 April 1931, 50-51. For the text of the 16 April speech see *Der Angriff* for 17 April, 1. For the naming of Schulz as Osaf-ost see Bessel, *Political Violence and the Rise of Nazism*, 63.

60. This interpretation of Hitler's role in the NSDAP is in agreement with Robert Koehl's "Feudal Aspects of National Socialism," in Henry A. Turner, Jr., ed., *Nazism and the Third Reich* (New York: Quadrangle, 1972), 154-74.

5. Appeals to the Proletariat

1. These statistics include both skilled and unskilled labor. Many in the former category were employed in the chemical industry and had as much in common with the middle classes as with the proletariat. See Wolfgang Bethge, *Berlins Geschichte im Ueberblick, 1237-1987.* (Berlin: Gebr. Holzapfel, 1987), 102.

2. Hamilton, *Who Voted for Hitler?*, 74. These statistics include the votes of the USPD, which was a participant in both elections of 1924, within the ranks of the other two working-class parties.

3. Among the best studies which see National Socialism as primarily an anti-modernist phenomenon are George L. Mosse, *The Crisis of German Ideology: Intellectual Origins of the Third Reich* (New York: Schocken, 1964); Robert Pois, *National Socialism and the Reli-*

gion of Nature (New York: Harper and Row, 1987); Ernst Nolte, *Der Faschismus in seiner Epoche: Action francaise, Italienischer Faschismus, Nationalsozialismus* (Munich: Piper, 1963). Zeev Sternhell's article, "Fascist Ideology," in *Fascism: A Reader's Guide: Analysis, Interpretation, Bibliography*, ed. Walter Laqueur (Berkeley: University of California Press, 1976), 315-76, while not dealing directly with National Socialism, sees fascism as a response to social and economic changes which occurred during the 1890s. For an overview of this debate, see Ian Kershaw, *The Nazi Dictatorship: Problems and Perspectives of Interpretation* (London: Edward Arnold, 1985), 26-30.

4. On the origin of the proletarian novel see Kele, *Nazis and Workers*, 111. Kele also outlines the plot and major themes of one of these serials, "From the Underworld," on pages 111-12.

5. See "Hans Sturms Erwachen," by Otto Baugert, in *Der Angriff*, 16 April 1928, 2.

6. Ibid.

7. Ibid.

8. Ibid.

9. Ibid.

10. Ibid.

11. "Hans Sturms Erwachen," by Otto Baugert, part two, *Der Angriff*, 23 April 1928, 2. Although the story does not name the speaker, it is clear it was Goebbels. "Lenin oder Hitler" was one of his most famous speeches.

12. Ibid.

13. Ibid.

14. Ibid.

15. Ibid.

16. Ibid.

17. Ibid., 14 May 1928, 1.

18. Ibid., 16 July 1928, 1.

19. Ibid., 20 August 1928, 5. A cartoon already discussed, "Heilige Opfer," also contributes to this theme. It shows several murdered SA men lying on the ground, an RFB man with a smoking pistol standing over them. Behind the RFB man is a Jew and the *Rote Fahne*. The Jews, the cartoonist claims, stand behind the "red murder."

20. Ibid., 16 July 1928, 5; emphasis in the original.

21. Ibid., 21 November 1929, 5.

22. "Immer wieder marxistischer Volksverrat," in *Der Angriff*, 14 May 1928, 1.

23. "Die S.P.D. fuer Kriegschuldluege!" in *Der Angriff*, 16 July 1928, 1.

24. "Die Reichsbahn macht Arbeitslose," in *Der Angriff*, 16 April 1928, 2.

25. "Standlose Arbeitszeiten bei der Post," in *Der Angriff*, 5 November 1928, 7.

26. "Gegen den Hugenberg-Kapitalismus; Gegen Standesduenkel und Klassenhass," in *Der Angriff*, Special Edition appearing in November 1932, 1.

27. Ibid., 2.

28. Henryk Skrzypczak, "'Revolutionaere' Gewerkschaftspolitik in der Weltwirtschaftskrise: Der Berliner Verkehrarbeiterstreik 1931," in *Gewerkschaftliche Monatshefte* 34, 4/5 (April-May 1983), 268; Hortzschansky, et al., *Ernst Thaelmann*, vol. 2, 621. For a brief historical overview of the BVG, see Henning Koehler, "Berlin in der Weimarer Republic (1918-1932)," in Wolfgang Ribbe, ed. *Geschichte Berlins*, vol. 2, *Von der Maerzrevolution bis zur Gegenwart* (Munich: Beck, 1987), 857-63.

29. Ben Fowkes, *Communism in Germany Under the Weimar Republic* (London: Macmillan, 1984), 168; Hortzschansky, et al., *Ernst Thaelmann*, 621. On the number of KPD led strikes in Germany, see Siegfried Bahne, "Die Kommunistische Partei Deutschlands," in Erich Matthias and Rudolf Morsey, eds., *Das Ende der Parteien 1933; Darstellungen und Dokumente* (Duesseldorf: Droste, 1960), 680. For a brief overview of trade union politics during the Weimar Republic, see Michael Schneider, "Zwischen Machtanspruch und Integrationsbereitschaft: Gewerkschaften und Politik 1918-1933," in Bracher, Funke, and Jacobsen, eds., *Die Weimarer Republik, 1918-1933*, 179-96.

30. Skrzypczak, "'Revolutionaere' Gewerkschaftspolitik," 265-69; Fowkes, *Communism in Germany*, 168.

31. Skrzypczak, "'Revolutionaere' Gewerkschaftpolitik," 269-70; Fowkes, *Communism in Germany*, 168; "Streikabstimmung bei der BVG," *Rote Fahne*, 2 November 1932, 9; "Keine Streikmehrheit bei der BVG.," in *Vorwaerts*, 3 November 1932, morning edition, 1.

32. On NSBO membership within the ranks of the BVG, see Skrzypczak, "'Revolutionaere' Gewerkschaftspolitik," 267. For Goebbels's view of the BVG strike, see Goebbels, *Tagebuecher*, vol. 2, 2 November 1932, 268. Hitler was in Berlin campaigning for the upcoming election, which provided Goebbels with the opportunity to convince his chief to support the transport workers. The date given in the *Tagebuecher* is undoubtedly incorrect since the 2 November entry records events which occurred on 3 November and even later. It is unclear whether this is a mistake on Goebbels's part which the editor failed to detect—she corrects dating mistakes in the manuscript when she finds them—or whether it is a mistake on the part of Froelich.

33. Ibid, 269; Skrzypczak, "'Revolutionaere' Gewerkschaftspo-

litik," 272; "Streik in der BVG!" in *Die Rote Fahne*, 3 November 1932, 1; "Teilverkehr in Berlin," in *Vorwaerts*, 5 November 1932, evening edition, 1.

34. "Zum Verkehrstreik," in *Vorwaerts*, 4 November 1932, morning edition, 1-2; "Putsch statt Streik" and "SA.-Putsch in Schoeneberg," both in *Vorwaerts*, 5 November 1932, morning edition, 1; "NSBO-Funktionaer brandmarkt die Streikbrecherrolle der Nazigauleitung" and "ADGB.-Fuehrer bereiten grosse Koalition mit Papen und Nazis vor," both in *Rote Fahne*, 3 November 1932, 6. On the prohibition of *Rote Fahne*, see "9 Tage verboten," in *Rote Fahne*, 4 November 1932, 1.

35. "Der Streik bei der BVG," in *Der Angriff*, 3 November 1932, 8.

36. Goebbels, *Tagebuecher*, vol. 2, 2 November 1932, 269; Engelbrechten, *Eine braune Armee entsteht*, 248; "Ein Todesopfer des Streiks!" in *Vorwaerts*, 4 November 1932, 1; "Schupo erschiesst SA.-Mann," in *Der Angriff*, 4 November 1932, 1.

37. Ibid.

38. "Unsere Volksgemeinschaft durch Blut geweiht," in *Der Angriff*, 4 November 1932, 1.

39. Ibid., 1-2.

40. "Verschaerfste Streiklage!" in *Der Angriff*, 5 November 1932, 2.

41. Skrzypczak, "'Revolutionaere' Gewerkschaftspolitik," 272-73; Engelbrechten and Volz, *Wir wandern durch das nationalsozialistische Berlin*, 46.

42. Oded Heilbronner comes to similar conclusions regarding the Black Forest region of Germany. He even goes so far as to state that "after a brief and relatively vigorous campaign in the countryside in the southern part of the Black forest in 1928, the peasantry was abandoned as a target of propaganda in favour of the working class." See Oded Heilbronner, "The Failure that Succeeded: Nazi Party Activity in a Catholic Region in Germany, 1929-1932," in *Journal of Contemporary History* 27 (July 1992): 542-43.

43. On this debate see Kershaw, *The Nazi Dictatorship*, 61-81. On *Der Stuermer* see Showalter, *Little Man, What Now?* It is important to note that many proponents of the "polycratic" view are much too quick to underestimate Hitler's power within the party or the Third Reich. For an example of Hitler's influence within the movement, see the discussion of his role in the Stennes Putsch in this work.

44. Michael Burleigh and Wolfgang Wippermann, *The Racial State: Germany, 1933-1945* (Cambridge: Cambridge University Press, 1991), 1. See also Thomas Childers, "The Social Language of Politics in Germany: The Sociology of Political Discourse in Weimar Germany," in *The American Historical Review* 95 (April 1990): 331-58.

45. Burleigh and Wippermann, *The Racial State*, 37. This is not
to suggest that National Socialism was not a revolutionary movement. As Burleigh and Wippermann show, Nazism was ultimately a
revolutionary form of racism, not only against Jews, but "Gypsies"
as well. They contend that, at the core of all Nazi policies, no matter
how "modern" or revolutionary, there was a persistent racism. The
goal of *all* Nazi policy was the creation of the *Volksgemeinschaft*, a
racist utopia. Concerning the antimodern nature of the "death
myth," see George Mosse, *Fallen Soldiers* (New York: Oxford Univ.
Press, 1990), 70-106.

6. The "System"

1. Articles attacking the "November Criminals" are numerous.
See, for example, "Das Gestaendnis der Verraeter," in *Der Angriff*, 27
April 1930, 1 and "Gegen Young und Bruening!" in *Der Angriff* 24
April 1930, 2.

2. "Parlamentarismus ist Korruption," in *Der Angriff*, 16 April
1928, 1; "Der Hoehepunkt des Steuerraubes!" in *Der Angriff*, 2 April
1928.

3. For an example of an article linking the Jews with the system, see "Jakob Goldschmidt als Wahlparole," in *Der Angriff*, 16
April 1928, 1. For examples of cartoons linking the Jews with the
system, see the cartoons "Gleiches Recht fuer Alle!??" in *Der Angriff*,
12 June 1930, 1; and "Skizzen aus dem Goebbels-Prozess," in *Der
Angriff*, 5 June 1930, 8.

4. Dietz Bering, "Von der Notwendigkeit politischer Beleidigungsprozesse: Der Beginn der Auseinandersetzung zwischen Poli-
zeivizepraesident Bernhard Weiss und der NSDAP," in Hans J. Reichhardt, ed., *Berlin in Geschichte und Gegenwart: Jahrbuch des Lan-
desarchivs Berlin* (1983), 87; Hsi-Huey Liang, *The Berlin Police Force in
the Weimar Republic* (Berkeley: University of California Press, 1970),
158-60; Rahm, *"Der Angriff,"* 48. Who first called Weiss "Isidor" is
unclear. Goebbels insisted that is was not he who invented the name,
and it is probable that, if he had, the Gauleiter would have been eager
to accept credit.

5. "Was bedeutet Isidor?" in *Der Angriff*, 31 October 1927, 3.

6. See "Verfassungsbruch der Berliner juedisch-marxistischen
Polizei," in *Voelkischer Beobachter*, 8/9 May 1927, 1; Bering, "Von der
Notwendigkeit politischer Beleidigungsprozesse," 87-108, passim.
For more about the legal battle between Weiss and the Berlin NSDAP,
see below.

7. For excellent examples of *Der Angriff's* caricatures of Weiss,

see *Der Angriff*, 15 August 1927, 1; 18 June 1928, 2; 14 May 1928, 5 and 28 November 1927, 5.

8. "Das Polizeipraesidium verordnet Hungerkuren" and "Der neue Nero," both in *Der Angriff*, 5 September 1927, 1, 5.

9. "Die Buettel des Herrn Isidor Mukiutschu," in *Der Angriff*, 26 September 1927, 7.

10. "Hilfe zugesagt und nicht gebracht," in *Der Angriff*, 1 June 1931, 9-10.

11. "Berliner Polizei in Theorie und Praxis," in *Der Angriff*, 15 April 1929, 10; "Skandal im Berliner Polizeipraesidium," *Der Angriff*, 5 December 1927, 1; "Nur an die Arbeit, Ihr Herren!" *Der Angriff*, 2 April 1928, 7.

12. See the cartoons in *Der Angriff*, 26 December 1927, 5; 19 September 1927, 5; and 15 September 1927, 1 respectively. For other examples of caricatures of Weiss, see chapter four.

13. Concerning the number of suits brought against *Der Angriff* by Weiss and others see Repositorium 58 in the Landesarchiv Berlin. This collection is probably incomplete. The number of suits brought against politically oriented newspapers, of both the left and right, became so great that, beginning in 1928, every prosecuting attorney had an assistant in charge of cases concerning the press. See "Der Preussische Justizminister ueber die Behandlung der Pressestrafsachen," in Repositorium 84a, Justizministerium Preussens, Aktum 4012, 77. For accounts of sanctions against the Communist Press, see file 223, box 21 of the German Subject Collection in the Hoover Institution Archives. A change in the Reich Press Law (1874) enacted in 1926 made editors legally responsible for articles printed in their papers. See "Entwurf eines Gesetzes zur Aenderung des Reichsgesetzes ueber die Presse vom 7. Mai 1874," in Repositorium 90, Bestimmungen ueber die Presse, Aktum 2412, Geheimes Staatsarchiv preussischer Kulturbesitz, 325-26. The change in the law was in response to KPD newspapers. On this see, Minister des Innern to Ministerpraesident, in Repositorium 90, Aktum 2412, 320.

14. See "Vorsicht! Gummiknueppel," in *Der Angriff* for 10 and 21 October, 28 November, and 5 December 1927, all on page 5. The cartoons in question can be found in *Der Angriff* for 28 November 1927, 5 and 10 October 1927, 5 respectively. On efforts of Weimar authorities to crush the RFB, see Schuster, *Der Rote Frontkaempferbund*, 193-238. In the end, these attempts proved as ineffective as those aimed at the SA.

15. "Strafsache gegen Duerr und Genossen," Aktum 24, Repositorium 58, Landesarchiv Berlin, 2-17. Goebbels, *Tagebuecher*, vol. 1, 28 April 1928, 219. Although the vast majority of suits against *Der*

Angriff were brought by such public figures as Weiss, Zoergiebel and Hindenburg, private citizens sometimes sued the paper for libel. See, for example, a suit brought by a legal firm for a story appearing in *Der Angriff*, "Juedische Anwaltsmethoden," in Repositorium 58, Aktum 18 in the Landesarchiv Berlin. Also, in cases where *Der Angriff* gave a byline for an article, the author was often brought up on charges. See the numerous cases brought against von Leers in his personnel file in the Berlin Document Center.

16. For examples of the first three techniques see numerous "Strafsachen," especially "Strafsache gegen Lippert," Aktum 18, Repositorium 58, 9; "Strafsache gegen Lippert," Aktum 7, Repositorium 58, 9-10, both in the Landesarchiv Berlin. For a case which Goebbels managed to drag out for over a year, see "Strafsache gegen Goebbels," Aktum 3, Repositorium 58, 14. His stalling tactics failed in the long run; he received a 1,000 RM fine (probably paid by the Gau). According to a newspaper article contained in the file for this case Goebbels had received 75 months in jail sentences in the previous three months alone.

17. "Gefaengnis fuer Dr. Goebbels," *Der Angriff*, 7 May 1928, 7.

18. See "Freispruch im Hindenburg-Prozess," *Der Angriff*, 5 June 1930, 4.

19. Reichsminister des Innern an die Obersten Reichs-und Landesbehoerden, 20 July 1931, in Repositorium 90, Aktum 2412, Geheimes Staatsarchiv, 367.

20. See the *Reichsgesetzblatt* for 28 March 1931, Repositorium 90, Aktum 2412, Geheimes Staatsarchiv, 347. For changes in the law made in 1932, see *Reichsgesetzblatt* for 16 June 1932, Repositorium 90, Aktum 2413, 11. Wolfgang Bretholz, "Zeitungsverbote," from the *Berliner Tageblatt*, 10 July 1931, in Repositorium 90, Aktum 2412, Geheimes Staatsarchiv, 352.

21. See Bretholz, "Zeitungsverbote;" "Der Angriff," in the NSDAP Hauptarchiv, Reel 47, Folder 968, 2.

22. *Verbot* issued against *Der Angriff* by the Polizeipraesident, 24 August 1932, Repositorium 43I, Kanzlei Rosenberg, Aktum 2533, Bundesarchiv, 250-54. For more information about the Beuthen case and the NSDAP's reaction to it, see Goebbels, *Tagebuecher*, vol. 2, 22-23 August 1932, 229-30. For Goebbels's brief mention of the prohibition, see his *Tagebuecher*, vol. 2, 25 August 1932, 230. Goebbels states that an "Attack against Herr von Papen" was the reason for the ban. The documentary evidence, however, shows that the grounds consisted of much more than an attack upon the Chancellor.

23. See for example, the single-page edition of *Der Angriff* appearing on 11 November 1930.

24. "Wir brauchen 1 000 RM," in the Hans Hinkel Collection, Hoover Institution Archives.

25. On the antimodern nature of anti-Semitism see Peter G.J. Pulzer, *The Rise of Political Anti-Semitism in Germany and Austria,* (New York: Wiley, 1964), 66, 240-41, 310-11; Fritz Stern, *The Politics of Cultural Despair: A Study in the Rise of the Germanic Ideology* (Berkeley: University of California Press, 1961), 62-63.

Conclusion

1. On this debate see Richard J. Evans, *In Hitler's Shadow: West German Historians and the Attempt to Escape from the Nazi Past* (New York: Pantheon, 1989), and Charles S. Maier, *The Unmasterable Past: History Holocaust, and German Identity* (Cambridge: Harvard University Press, 1988). For a collection of some the most important texts to emerge during the dispute, known as the "Historikerstreit," see *"Historikerstreit:" Die Dokumentation der Krontroverse um die Einzigartigkeit der nationalsozialistischen Judenvernichtung* (Munich: Piper, 1987).

Bibliography

PRIMARY SOURCES

Archives

Berlin Document Center
Various Personnel Files

Bundesarchiv, Koblenz
NS 8 Kanzlei Rosenberg
NS 18 Reichspropagandaleiter
NS 22 Reichsorganisationsleiter
NS 23 SA Archiv
R 43 Reichskanzlei
Sammlung Schumacher

Geheimes Staatsarchiv Preussischer Kulturbesitz, Berlin
Rep. 84a Justizministerium
Rep. 90 Bestimmungen ueber die Presse
Zeitgeschichtliche Sammlung

The Hoover Institution on War, Revolution and Peace, Stanford, California
Hans Hinkel Collection
German Subject Collection
NSDAP Hauptarchiv (Microfilm)

Institut fuer Zeitgeschichte, Munich
ED 188 Otto Strasser Sammlung

Landesarchiv Berlin
Rep. 58 Akten des Generalstaatanwalts beim Landgericht Berlin
Rep. 240 Zeitgeschichtliche Sammlung

Library of Congress
Hartmann, Franz. "Statistische und geschichtliche Entwicklung der
   NS Presse, 1926-1935." Unpublished Manuscript. Munich, 1936.

Newspapers

Der Angriff, Berlin.
Berliner Arbeiter Zeitung, Berlin.
Rote Fahne, Berlin.
Voelkischer Beobachter, Munich.
Vorwaerts, Berlin.

Published Primary Sources

Bade, Wilfred. *Die SA erobert Berlin. Eine Tatsachenbericht*. Munich,
   1934.
Behrendt, Erich F. *Soldaten der Freiheit*. Berlin, 1935.
Birn, Hermann. *Nur eine Schar SA*. Berlin, 1936.
Boelcke, Willi A., ed. *Kriegspropaganda 1939-1941: Geheime Minis-
   terkonferenzen im Reichspropagandaministerium*. Stuttgart, 1966.
Broszat, Martin, ed. "Die Anfaenge der Berliner NSDAP 1926/27." In
   Vierteljahrshefte fuer Zeitgeschichte 8 (January 1960): 85-118.
Bruening, Heinrich. *Memoiren, 1918-1934*. Stuttgart, 1970.
Dietrich, Otto. *12 Jahre mit Hitler*. Munich, 1955.
Engelbrechten, J.K. *Eine braune Armee entsteht. Die Geschichte der
   Berlin-Brandenburger SA*. Munich, 1937.
———. *Wir wandern durch das nationalsozialistische Berlin*. Munich,
   1937.
Goebbels, Joseph. *Kampf um Berlin: Der Anfang, 1926-1927*. Munich,
   1932.
———. *My Part in Germany's Fight*. Trans. by K. Fiedler. New York,
   1979.
———. *Die Tagebuecher von Joseph Goebbels: Saemtliche Fragmente*. 4
   vols. Elke Froelich, ed. Munich, 1987.
———. *Vom Kaiserhof zur Reichskanzlei*. Munich, 1937.
———. and "Mjoelnir." *Das Buch Isidor*. Munich, 1928.
Halbmast: Ein Heldenbuch der SA und SS. Berlin, 1932.
Heiber, Helmut, ed. *The Early Goebbels Diaries: The Journal of Joseph
   Goebbels from 1925-1926*. London, 1962.
*"Historikerstreit: Die Dokumentation der Kontroverse um die Einzigar-
   tigkeit der nationalsozialistischen Judenvernichtung."* Munich,
   1987.
Hitler, Adolf. *Mein Kampf*. Trans. by R. Mannheim. New York, 1943.
"Horst Wessel, 'Feierabend' Heft 5." Leipzig, n.d.
Killinger, Manfred von. *Die SA im Wort und Bild*. Leipzig, 1933.

Klagges, Dietrich. *Kampf dem Marxismus.* Munich, 1930.
Koch, Karl. *Maenner im Braunhemd. Vom Kampf und Sieg der* SA. Duesseldorf, 1936.
Matthias, Erich, and Rudolf Morsey, eds. *Das Ende der Parteien 1933: Darstellungen und Dokumente.* Duesseldorf, 1960.
Severing, Carl. *Mein Lebensweg.* 2 vols. Cologne, 1950.
Stark, G. *Moderne politische Propaganda.* Munich, 1930.
Strasser, Otto. *Hitler and I.* Boston, 1940.
Sturm 33: Hans Maikowski. Geschrieben von Kameraden des Toten. Berlin, 1934.
Turner, Henry Ashby, Jr., ed. *Hitler: Memoirs of a Confidant.* Trans. by R. Hein. New Haven, 1985.
Wessel, Ingeborg. *Mein Bruder Horst. Ein Vermaechtnis.* Munich, 1934.

SECONDARY SOURCES

Abel, Theodore. *Why Hitler Came Into Power.* Cambridge, Mass., 1986.
Baird, Jay W. "Goebbels, Horst Wessel, and the Myth of Resurrection and Return." *Journal of Contemporary History* 17 (October 1982): 633-49.
————. *The Mythical World of Nazi War Propaganda, 1939-1945.* Minneapolis, 1974.
————. *To Die for Germany: Heroes in the Nazi Pantheon.* Bloomington, 1990.
Bering, Dietz. "Von der Notwendigkeit politischer Beleidigungsprozesse: Der Beginn der Auseindersetzung zwischen Polizei-vizepraesident Bernhard Weiss und der NSDAP." In Hans J. Reichhardt, ed., *Berlin in Geschichte und Gegenwart.* Berlin, 1983, 87-112.
Bessel Richard. *Political Violence and the Rise of Nazism: The Storm Troopers in Eastern Germany, 1925-1934.* New Haven, 1984.
Bethge, Wolfgang. *Berlins Geschichte im Ueberblick, 1237-1987.* Berlin, 1987.
Boelcke, Willi A. *"Wollt Ihr den totalen Krieg?" Die geheimen Goebbelskonferenzen, 1939-1945.* Stuttgart, 1966.
Bracher, K.D. *Die Aufloesung der Weimarer Republik.* Stuttgart, 1955.
————. *The German Dictatorship: The Origins, Structure and Effects of National Socialism.* New York, 1970.
Bramsted, Ernest, K. *Goebbels and National Socialist Propaganda, 1925-1945.* East Lansing, Mich., 1965.
Breitman, Richard. *German Socialism and Weimar Democracy.* Chapel Hill, 1981.

Broszat, Martin. *Hitler and the Collapse of Weimar Germany*. Trans. by V.R. Berghahn. New York, 1987.

Brown, Jeremy R.S. "The Berlin NSDAP in the *Kampfzeit*." *German History* 7 (August 1989): 241-47.

Bullock, Alan. *Adolf Hitler: A Study in Tyranny*. New York, 1951.

Burleigh, Michael and Wippermann, Wolfgang. *The Racial State: Germany, 1933-1945*. Cambridge, 1991.

Carsten, F.L. *The Reichswehr and Politics, 1918-1933*. Berkeley, 1973.

———. *The Rise of Fascism*. Berkeley, 1967.

Childers, Thomas. *The Nazi Voter: The Social Foundations of Fascism in Germany, 1919-1933*. Chapel Hill, 1983.

———. "The Social Language of Politics in Germany: The Sociology of Political Discourse in Weimar Germany." *American Historical Review* 95 (April 1990): 331-58.

Cohnstaedt, W. "German Newspapers Before Hitler." *Journalism Quarterly* 12 (June 1935): 157-63.

Combs, William L. *The Voice of the SS: A History of the SS Journal "Das Schwarze Korps."* New York, 1986.

Diehl, James. *Paramilitary Politics in Weimar Germany*. Bloomington, 1977.

Dominick, Raymond H., III. *Wilhelm Liebknecht and the Founding of the German Social Democratic Party*. Chapel Hill, 1982.

Dorpalen, Andreas. *Hindenburg and the Weimar Republic*. Princeton, 1964.

Eksteins, Modris. *The Limits of Reason: The German Democratic Press and the Collapse of Weimar Democracy*. London, 1975.

Evans, Richard J. *In Hitler's Shadow: West German Historians and the Attempt to Escape from the Nazi Past*. New York, 1989.

Eyck, Erich. *A History of the Weimar Republic*. 2 vols. Trans. by H.P. Hanson and R.G.L. Waite. Cambridge, Mass., 1963.

Falter, Juergen W. "Wahlen und Wahlenverhalten unter besonderer Beruecksichtigung des Augsteiges der NSDAP nach 1928." Karl Dietrich Bracher, Manfred Funke and Hans-Adolf Jacobsen, eds. *Die Weimarer Republik, 1918-1933: Politik, Wirtschaft, Gesellschaft*. Duesseldorf, 1987, 484-504.

Fest, Joachim. *Hitler*. New York, 1975.

Fischer, Conan. *The German Communists and the Rise of Nazism*. New York, 1991.

———. *Stormtroopers: A Social, Economic and Ideological Analysis, 1929-1935*. London, 1983.

Flood, Charles Bracelen. *Hitler: The Path to Power*. Boston, 1989.

Fowkes, Ben. *Communism in Germany Under the Weimar Republic*. New York, 1984.

Frei, Norbert, and Johannes Schmitz. *Journalismus im Dritten Reich*. Munich, 1989.

Gleich, Oliver. "Die Spandauer SA 1926 bis 1933." In Wolfgang Ribbe, ed., *Berlin-Forschungen III*. Berlin, 1988.

Hale, Oron J. *The Captive Press in the Third Reich*. Princeton, 1964.

Hamilton, Richard. *Who Voted for Hitler?* Princeton, 1982.

Hannover, Heinrich, and Elisabeth Hannover-Drueck. *Politische Justiz, 1918-1933*. Frankfurt/M, 1966.

Heiber, Helmut. *Joseph Goebbels*. Stuttgart, 1965.

Heiden, Konrad. *Der Fuehrer: Hitler's Rise to Power*. Trans. by R. Mannheim. Boston, 1944.

Heilbronner, Oded. "The Failure that Succeeded: Nazi Party Activity in a Catholic Region in Germany, 1929-1932." *Journal of Contemporary History* 27 (July 1992): 531-49.

Herzstein, Robert Edwin. *The War That Hitler Won: Goebbels and the Nazi Media Campaign*. New York, 1978.

Hoehne, Heinz. *The Order of the Death's Head: The Story of Hitler's SS*. New York, 1971.

Horn, Wolfgang. *Der Marsch zur Machtergreifung: Die NSDAP bis 1933*. Duesseldorf, 1980.

Hortzchansky, Guenter, et al. *Ernst Thaelmann: Eine Biographie*. 2 vol. paperback edition. East Berlin, 1985.

Huettenberger, Peter. *Die Gauleiter: Studie zum Wandel des Machtgefueges in der NSDAP*. Stuttgart, 1969.

Jablonsky, David. "Roehm and Hitler: The Continuity of Political-Military Discord." In *Journal of Contemporary History* 23 (July 1988): 367-85.

Kater, Michael. "Ansaetze zu einer Soziologie der SA bis zur Roehm-Krise." In Ulrich Engelhardt, V. Sellin and H. Stuke, eds. *Soziale Bewegung und politische Verfassung*. Stuttgart, 1976, 798-831.

———. *The Nazi Party: A Social Profile of Members of Leaders, 1919-1945*. Cambridge, Mass., 1983.

———. "The Revenge of the Fathers: The Demise of Modern Music at the End of the Weimar Republic." *German Studies Review* 15 (May 1992): 295-316.

———. "Zum gegenseitigen Verhaeltnis von SA und SS in der Sozialgeschichte des Nationalsozialismus von 1925 bis 1939." In *Vierteljahrsschrift fuer Sozial-und Wirtschafts-geschichte* 62 (1975): 339-79.

Kaupert, Walter. *Die Deutsche Tagespresse als Politicum*. Freudenstadt, 1932.

Kele, Max H. *Nazis and Workers: National Socialist Appeals to German Labor*. Chapel Hill, 1972.

Kenez, Peter. *The Birth of the Propaganda State: Soviet Methods of Mass Mobilization, 1917-1929.* Cambridge, 1985.

Kershaw, Ian. *The Hitler Myth: Image and Reality in the Third Reich.* Oxford, 1987.

———. *The Nazi Dictatorship: Problems and Perspectives of Interpretation.* London, 1985.

———. *Popular Opinion and Political Dissent in the Third Reich: Bavaria, 1933-1945.* Oxford, 1983.

Koehl, Robert. "Feudal Aspects of National Socialism." Henry A. Turner, Jr., ed. *Nazism and the Third Reich.* New York, 1972, 154-74.

Koonz, Claudia. *Mothers in the Fatherland: Women, the Family and Nazi Politics.* New York, 1987.

Kuehnl, Reinhard. *Die Nationalsozialistische Linke 1925-1930.* Meisenheim/Glan, 1966.

———. "Zur Programmatik der Nationalsozialistischen Linken: Das Strasser-Program von 1925/26." *Vierteljahrshefte fuer Zeitgeschichte* 14 (July 1966): 317-33.

Layton, Ronald V. "The *Voelkischer Beobachter*, 1920-1933: The Nazi Newspaper in the Weimar Era." *Central European History* 3 (1970): 353-82.

Lazar, Imre. *Der Fall Horst Wessel.* Stuttgart, 1980.

Liang, Hsi-huey. *The Berlin Police Force in the Weimar Republic.* Berkeley, 1970.

Longreich, Peter. *Die braunen Bataillone: Geschichte der SA.* Munich, 1989.

McKale, Donald. *The Nazi Party Courts: Hitler's Management of Conflict in His Movement, 1921-1945.* Lawrence, Kans., 1974.

Maier, Charles S. *The Unmasterable Past: History, Holocaust and German National Identity.* Cambridge, Mass., 1988.

Manvell, Roger, and Heinrich Fraenkel. *Dr. Goebbels: His Life and Death.* New York, 1960.

Mendelssohn, Peter de. *Zeitungstadt Berlin. Menschen und Maechte der Geschichte der deutschen Presse.* Berlin, 1959.

Merkl, Peter. *The Making of a Stormtrooper.* Princeton, 1980.

Mitchell, Otis. "An Institutional History of the National Socialist SA: A Study of the SA as a Functioning Organization within the Party Structure (1931-1934)." Ph.D. dissertation, University of Kansas, 1972.

Mosse, George L. *The Crisis of German Ideology: Intellectual Origins of the Third Reich.* New York, 1966.

———. *Fallen Soldiers.* Oxford, 1989.

Niewyk, Donald L. *Socialist, Anti-Semite and Jew: German Social De-*

mocracy Confronts the Problem of Anti-Semitism, 1918-1933. Baton Rouge, 1971.

Nolte, Ernst. *Der Faschismus in seiner Epoche*. Munich, 1963.

Orlow, Dietrich. *The History of the Nazi Party, 1919-1933*. Pittsburgh, 1969.

————. Weimar *Prussia, 1918-1925: The Unlikely Rock of Democracy*. Pittsburgh, 1986.

Plieninger, Martin. "Die Kampfpresse: Ein neuer Zeitungstyp." *Zeitungswissenschaft* 2 (March 1933): 65-75.

Pois, Robert. *National Socialism and the Religion of Nature*. New York, 1987.

Pulzer, G.J. *The Rise of Political Anti-Semitism in Germany and Austria*. New York, 1964.

Raehm, Hans-Georg. *"Der Angriff," 1927-1930: Der nationalsozialistische Typ der Kampfzeit*. Berlin, 1939.

Reimann, Viktor. *Dr. Joseph Goebbels*. Vienna, 1971.

Ribbe, Wolfgang, ed. *Geschichte Berlins*. 2 vols. Munich, 1987.

Rosenhaft, Eve. *Beating the Fascists? The German Communists and Political Violence*. Cambridge, 1983.

Schneider, Michael. "Zwischen Machtanspruch und Integrationsbereitschaft: Gewerkschaften und Politik 1918-1933." In Bracher, Funke, and Jacobsen, eds. *Die Weimarer Republik, 1918-1933*. Stuttgart, 1987, 179-96.

Schuddekopf, Otto-Ernst. *Nationalbolschewismus in Deutschland, 1918-1933*. Frankfurt/M, 1972.

Shirer, William L. *The Rise and Fall of the Third Reich: A History of Nazi Germany*. New York, 1959.

Showalter, Dennis. *Little Man What Now? "Der Stuermer" in the Weimar Republic*. New York, 1986.

Skrzypczak, Henryk. "'Revolutionaere' Gewerkschaftspolitik in der Weltwirtschaftskrise: Der Berliner Verkehrarbeiterstreik 1932." *Gewerkschaftliche Monatshefte* 34, 4/5 (April-May 1983): 264-77.

Stachura, Peter. "Der kritische Wendepunkt? Die NSDAP und die Reichstagwahlen vom 20. Mai 1928." In *Vierteljahrshefte fuer Zeitgeschichte* 26 (1978): 66-99.

————. *Gregor Strasser and the Rise of Nazism*. London, 1983.

————. "The Nazis, the Bourgeoisie and the Workers during the *Kampfzeit*." Peter Stachura, ed. *The Nazi Machtergreifung*. London, 1983, 13-40.

————. "The Political Strategy of the Nazi Party, 1919-1933." *German Studies Review* 3 (May 1980): 261-88.

Stein, Peter. *Die NS Gaupresse, 1925-1933*. Munich, 1987.

Stern, Fritz. *The Politics of Cultural Despair: A Study in the Rise of the Germanic Ideology*. Berkeley, 1961.

Sternhell, Zeev. "Fascist Ideology." Walter Laqueur, ed. *Fascism: A Reader's Guide: Analysis, Interpretation, Bibliography.* Berkeley, 1976, 315-76.

Toland, John. *Adolf Hitler.* New York, 1977.

Treviranus, Gottfried Reinhold. *Das Ende von Weimar: Heinrich Bruening und seine Zeit.* Duesseldorf, 1968.

Turner, Henry Ashby, Jr. *German Big Business and the Rise of Hitler.* New York, 1985.

Ward, James J. "'Smash the Fascists . . . ' German Communist Efforts to Counter the Nazis, 1930-1931." *Central European History* 14 (March 1981): 30-62.

Welch, David. *Propaganda and the German Cinema, 1933-1945.* Oxford: 1983.

Werner, Andreas. "SA der NSDAP. SA: 'Wehrverband,' 'Parteitruppe' oder 'Revolutionsarmee'? Studien zur Geschichte der SA und der NSDAP bis 1933." Ph.D. dissertation, University of Erlangen, 1964.

Wheeler-Bennet, John W. *Wooden Titan: Hindenburg in Twenty Years of German History, 1914-1934.* New York, 1936.

Wilcox, Larry. "The National Socialist Party Press in the 'Kampfzeit,' 1919-1933." Ph.D. dissertation, University of Virginia, 1970.

————. "The Nazi Press in the Third Reich: *Voelkisch Presse, Kampfblaetter, Gauzeitungen.*" In F.J. Homer and Larry D. Wilcox, eds., *Germany and Europe in the Era of the Two World Wars: Essays in Honor of Oron Hale.* Charlottesville, 1986, 79-119.

Wippermann, Wolfgang. "Aufsteig der NSDAP in Berlin." Unpublished manuscript.

Zeman, Z.A.B. *Nazi Propaganda.* London, 1964.

Index

Amann, Max, 34-36, 39, 45, 86-87, 152 n 57

Angriff, Der, 2, 128-31; administration of, 37-38; and aerial campaign tour, 62-63; anti-Semitism in, 2, 5, 24, 32-33, 52-53, 60, 68, 70, 74, 79, 91, 94, 117, 118-19, 120-21, 126-27, 129, 157 n 13, 158 n 15; becomes daily, 34-36, 49, 90, 139-40 n 33; becomes official Gau organ, 44, 48-49; becomes ten pages, 34; becomes twelve pages, 33; and Berlin Police, 112-23 *passim*; circulation of, 38, 39, 40-41, 42, 125, 129, 139-40 n 33; columns in, 32-34; creation of, 21-25; distribution of, 30-31, 139-40 n 33; financial condition of, 38-40, 125-26; first issue of, 24-25; and "Fuehrer Myth," 53-63, 129; and Goebbels-Strasser dispute, 44-49; and Horst Wessel, 2, 73-75, 129; layout of, 31-34; libel actions against, 120-23, 157 n 13, 158 n 15; and political violence, 65-68, 95; prohibitions of, 120, 124-26; proletarian novels in, 90-95, 140 n 40; and proletariat, 41-42, 89-110, 116, 129; quality of, 31, 38; readership of, 40-42; staff of, 25-30, 50, 69, 108, 122; and

Stennes Revolt, 80-88 *passim*; and Weimar "System," 111-27; *see also,* Goebbels, Joseph
Angriff Verlag, 36
Assmann, Eberhard, 28

Baird, Jay W., 1; and "myth of resurrection and return," 72-73
Bamberg leadership conference. *See* Goebbels, Joseph
Baugert, Otto, 90
Berlin, 3, 65, 68, 70, 71, 72, 73, 77, 80, 81, 84, 85, 90, 92, 94, 95, 102, 108, 128, 129, 131; police force of, 51, 68-69, 71, 76, 77, 80, 86, 105-6, 112-20, 126; as proletarian city, 89-90, 152 n 1
Berliner Arbeiter Zeitung (BAZ), 23, 32, 43-49
Berliner Lokal-Anzeiger, 102
Berliner Morgenpost, 16
Berliner Tageblatt, 24
Berlin Transportation Corporation (BVG), 102-8, 154 n 32
Berlin, University of, 72
Beuthen, 124
"Black Reichswehr," 81
Boelcke, W.A., 1
Bramsted, Ernest K., 1, 5
Brandenburg, 85
Bretholz, Wolfgang, 124

Brown, Jeremy, 41-42
Bruening, Heinrich, 56-57, 61, 64
Burleigh, Michael, 109, 110

Chamberlain, Houston Stewart, 53-54
Chicago, 89
Combs, William, 1

Daleuge, Kurt, 8, 16, 85
Dawes Plan, 100, 111, 112
Dornbusch, Frau, 117
Dresden, 63, 84
Duerr, Dagobert, 26, 120, 121, 122
Duesseldorf, 83
Duesterberg, Theodor, 58, 60, 62

Egypt, 113
Eher Verlag. See Amann, Max
Enlightenment, 110
Entente Powers, 111

Felseneck, 76
Fischer, Walter, 70-71, 74
Frankfurt, 63
Frei, Norbert, 1
Friedrichshain, 73
Frohnau, 75
Frontbann. See Sturmabteilung

German Communist Party (KPD), 2, 7, 15, 17, 86, 89, 90, 109, 110; and BVG strike, 103-8 passim; in Nazi propaganda, 91-110 passim; in 1932 presidential campaign, 56, 58, 59-64; and political violence, 65-79 passim
German Democratic Party (DDP), 115
Germania, 22
German Labor Front, 128
German Social Democratic Party (SPD), 22, 60, 67, 89, 90, 99-100, 101, 111, 118; and BVG strike, 103-8 passim
German Trade Union Federation (ADGB), 103

Goebbels, Joseph, 2, 3, 4, 8, 102, 109, 113, 127, 128, 131; and administration of Der Angriff, 37-38; and aerial campaign tour, 62; anti-Semitism of, 19, 52-53; articles of, in Der Angriff, 49, 51-53, 62, 73-74, 107; becomes Berlin Gauleiter, 9-11; becomes Hitler supporter, 9-10; and Bernhard Weiss, 113-14, 120, 121-22; and BVG strike, 104-7; and circulation of Der Angriff, 40-41, 42; and "conquest" of Berlin, 89; and creation of Der Angriff, 21-25; diaries of, 82, 85, 87, 125, 154 n 32; and efforts to make Der Angriff a daily, 34-36; and feud with Strassers, 23-24, 129; and financial condition of Der Angriff, 38-40; and "Fuehrer Myth," 53-63; at mass rallies, 15-16, 18-19, 57, 92; and Michael, 36; and 1932 presidential campaign, 57-62; opinions of Der Angriff, 31; as party propaganda chief, 57-59; and "Political Diary," 32, 47-48; and political violence, 65, 73-74, 118; and the press as propaganda tool, 36-37, 39; and prohibition of NSDAP, 19-20; and Redeverbot, 20, 38-39; and reorganization of Berlin NSDAP, 12-13; and response to court cases, 122-24; and SA, 13; special powers of, 11, 82; and staff of Der Angriff, 25-30, 89, 108; and Stennes Revolt, 80-88
Goering, Hermann, 83, 86
Grzenski, Albert, 19
Guenz, Herbert, 117

Hageinan (leader of Court of Honor), 8
Hale, Oron, 1, 3
"Hans Sturm's Awakening," 90-95
"Harzburg Front," 58
Heiber, Helmut, 5

Heider, A., 100
Herzstein, Robert, 1
Hess, Rudolf, 34
Hess, Willi, 83
Hindenburg, Otto, 55-64, 123
Hinkel, Hans, 28, 87, 126
Hitler, Adolf, 1, 7, 9, 34, 78, 99, 109, 130; becomes German Chancellor, 128; and Goebbels-Strasser dispute, 24, 43-49; and 1932 presidential campaign, 55-64; speaks in Berlin, 18, 54-55; and Stennes Revolt, 80-88 *passim*
Hitler Youth, 76-78
Hoehler, Ali, 72-73
Hoehne (police commissar), 117
Hugenberg, Alfred, 56, 101, 102

Interior, Ministry of, 124, 125

Jaenicke, Erna, 72
Jahn, Wilhelm, 84
Joffre, Field Marshal Joseph, 100
Journal of Italy, 55
Justice, Ministry of, 124

Kampfgemeinschaft revolutionaerer Nationalsozialisten ("Black Front"), 46-47, 86
Kampfverlag. *See* Strasser, Gregor
Kampfzeit (Time of Struggle), 1, 32, 33, 129
Kampfzeitung (fighting newspaper), 21-22
Kampmann, Karoly, 29
Kater, Michael, 42, 66
Kershaw, Ian, 1
Kirsch, Johannes, 76-77
Knodn (acting Gauleiter of Berlin), 8
Koch, Erich, 23
Krause, Willi, 29
Kreuzberg, 6
Kurfuerstendamm, 17

Leers, Johann von, 30
Lippert, Julius, 21, 24, 71; back-ground of, 25; as editor in chief of *Der Angriff*, 25-26, 38, 120
London, 89
Ludendorff, Erich, 8
Luxemburg, Rosa, 102

Marxism, 52, 61, 68, 75, 79, 93, 94, 99, 110, 111, 113, 126, 130; see also German Communist Party and German Social Democratic Party
Middle Ages, 110
Mitarbeiter (associates), 30
"Mjoelnir." *See* Schweitzer, Hans
Moabit, 76
Mosse, George, 109
Mueller, Adolf, 34-35
Munich, 9, 11, 80, 84, 87

Nationalist Party, 56, 62
National Socialist German Workers' Party (NSDAP), 2, 18, 65, 68, 69, 72, 80, 91, 97, 113-14, 117, 118, 123, 129, 130, 131; and BVG strike, 104-8; compared with early Christianity, 50, 74-75, 79, 116; electoral breakthrough of, 41; established in Berlin, 6-7; factionalism in, 8, 46-47, 88, 109; Hitler centrist v. polycratic view of, 109, 155 n 43; ideology of, 3, 51-53, 85, 90, 104, 106-7, 109-10, 126-127, 130-31, 153 n 3, 156 n 45; and 1932 presidential campaign, 55-64; and peasantry, 44, 155 n 42; prohibited in Berlin, 6-7, 19-20, 39, 49-51, 66, 116; and proletariat, 41-42, 44, 76, 89-110 *passim*, 155 n 42; propaganda of, 3, 53; and Reichstag elections, 89, 108, 115
National Socialist Organization of Shop Stewards (NSBO), 104, 105
National Socialist Women's Organization, 34
Nationalsozialist, Der, 45, 47
Nationalsozialistische Kampf-

bewegung Deutschlands (NSKD),
86, 152 n 54
Neukoelln, 14
New York City, 89
Nolte, Ernst, 131
Norkus, Herbert, 76-78, 79
"November Criminals," 2, 60, 111;
see also "System"
NS-Briefe, 23
Nuremberg, 65, 116
Nuremberg Party Congresses,
49-50, 53-54, 115-16

Oberbayrischen Tageszeitung, 28

Papen, Franz von, 105
Pfeffer, Franz, 80-82
Pharussaele, 15, 17
political violence, 14, 65-79; see
also Sturmabteilung
Pomerania, 85, 124
Post Office, 101
Potsdam, 63
Prussia, 124
Pulzer, Peter, 126

Raehm, Hans-Georg
Rathenau, Walther, 6
Reich Press Law, 120, 123-24
Reichsbahn, 100-101
Reichsbanner, 66-67, 68, 97
Reichsbanner, 55
"Reichskanzler" (restaurant), 6
Reichstag, 89, 112, 115
Reinickendorf, 75, 76
Reppich, Kurt, 105-7
Roehm, Ernst, 7, 83, 85
Rote Fahne, 17, 18, 22, 47, 72, 74,
99, 104-5, 153 n 19; compared
with Der Angriff, 27
Rotfrontkaempferbund (RFB), 2, 3,
91, 97, 117, 121; and clashes with
SA, 14-17, 67, 69-71, 75
Ruprecht, Philip ("Fips"), 27-28

Saechsischer Beobachter, 45
Scherl-Verlag, 101-2

Schlange, Ernst, 7
Schlossbrauerei Schoneberg, 68, 69
Schmiedecke, Erich, 8
Schmitz, Johannes, 1
Schulz, Paul, 87
Schulze, Hans, 24, 121
Schutzstaffel (SS), 15, 82, 85
Schwartz, Ernst, 67, 75-76
Schweitzer, Hans, background of,
26-27; and Bernhard Weiss, 27;
as cartoonist, 27-28, 44, 50, 54,
59-60, 67, 74, 95-99, 115, 118-19,
121; compared with Philip
Ruprecht ("Fips"), 27-28; and
Goebbels, 27, 38; as "Mjoelnir,"
27-28
Severing, Carl, 6-7
Showalter, Dennis, 1
Silesia, 83, 85
Soviet Union, 1, 55, 130
Spandau, 14
Sportpalast, 57, 63, 87
Stahlhelm, 62
Stalin, Joseph, 1, 130
Stein, Peter, 1-2
Stennes, Walther, 28, 80-88 passim
Strasser, Gregor, 32; and dispute
with Goebbels, 23-24, 43-49; and
Kampfverlag, 9, 36
Strasser, Otto, 9, 32, 86, 108; and
dispute with Goebbels, 23-24,
43-49
Streicher, Julius, 6, 27, 109
Stresemann, Gustav, 32
Sturmabteilung (SA), 2, 3, 65-88, 91,
116; and BVG strike, 105-7; and
clashes with RFB, 14-17; composi-
tion of, 66-67, 146 n 3; creation of,
in Berlin, 7-8; and distribution of
Der Angriff, 30; and Frontbann,
7-8; and Goebbels-Strasser dispute, 43, 44, 45; as martyrs,
70-76, 79-80, 105-6, 153 n 19; organization of, 151 n 44; and parades,
13, 54; and political violence,
65-77, 92-93, 95, 147 n 13; as propaganda troop, 13, 65; and

Stennes Revolt, 77-88, 150 n 38;
and weapons, 18
Stuermer, Der, 27-28, 65, 109
Switzerland, 100
"System," 48, 59, 60, 70, 71, 77; in
Der Angriff, 111-27, 129

Tannenberg, Battle of, 59
Tannenbergbund. *See* Ludendorff,
Erich
Thaelmann, Ernst, 55, 58, 60, 62, 64
Thimm, Erich, 7
Turnerschaften, 7

"urban plan," 10, 44

Versailles, Treaty of, 32, 64, 81, 100,
102, 111
Voelkischer Beobachter, 22, 24, 39;
Berlin edition of, 34-35, 45
Volksgemeinschaft, 85, 107, 110, 131
Vorwaerts, 22, 99, 104
Vossische Zeitung, 24

Wartzburgplatz, 106
Wedding, 15

Weimar, 10, 84
Weimar Republic, 3, 4, 41, 50, 71,
94, 95, 101, 111, 123, 127, 129, 130;
see also "System"
Weiss, Bernhard, 50; in *Der Angriff,*
112-17, 118-22; as "Isidor," 113,
118, 120, 129; and legal action
against *Der Angriff,* 114, 115,
120-23, 126; as "New Nero," 116;
as symbol of the "System,"
119-26
Weissauer, Ludwig, 28, 85, 87
Welsh, David, 1
Welt am Abend, 16, 17, 24
Wessel, Horst, 2, 71-75, 129
Wetzel, Bruno, 84
Wiedemann, Melitta, 28-29
Wilmersdorf, 70
Wippermann, Wolfgang, 109, 110
Wolf (Berlin SS chief), 8
Worldwide depression, 66, 129

Young Plan, 111

Zoergiebel, Karl, 19, 59